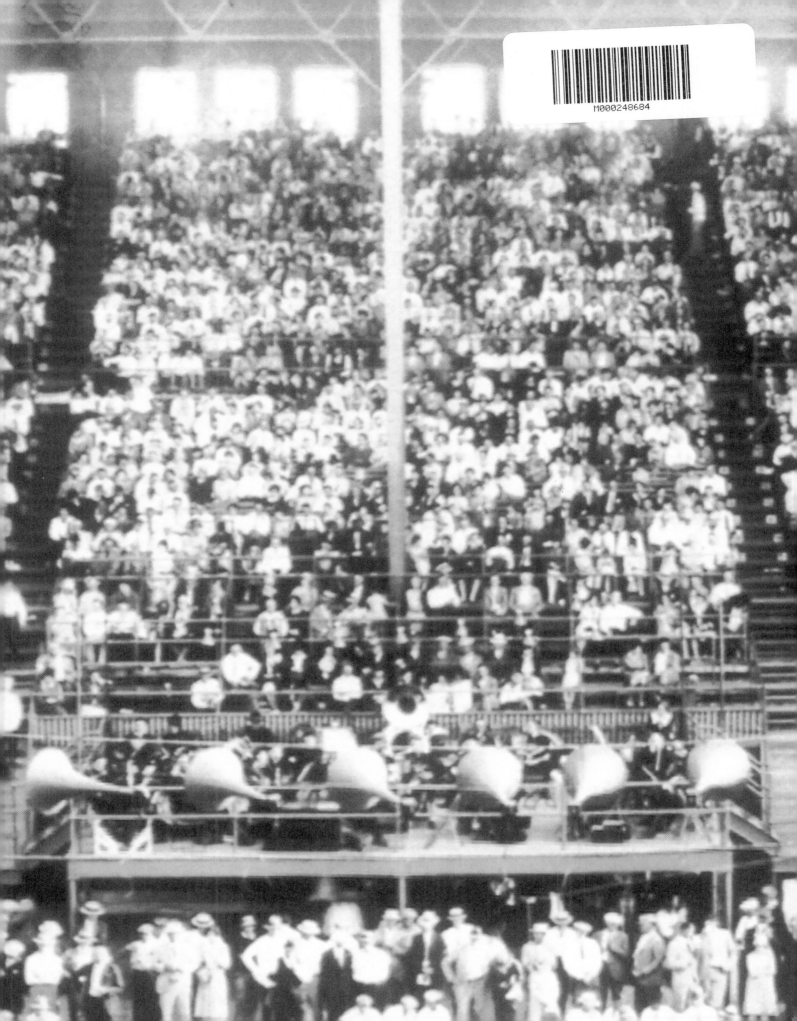

Our State Fair
Iowa's Blue Ribbon Story

Written by
MARY KAY SHANLEY

Designed by
PAUL MICICH ILLUSTRATION

IOWA STATE FAIR
BLUE RIBBON
FOUNDATION

© 2000 Iowa State Fair Blue Ribbon Foundation
666 Grand Avenue, Suite 1717, Des Moines, Iowa 50309
Printed by Sigler Printing & Publishing
413 Northwestern, Ames, Iowa 50010
ISBN 1-888223-17-0

ACKNOWLEDGEMENTS

It would be great if we could thank every single person who ever helped assemble an Iowa State Fair or attended one! After all, these people are the reason for this book. From that first humble Fair in Fairfield back in 1854 to the extravaganzas we enjoy today, the Iowa State Fair always has been a celebration of Iowa and its people. Still, listing everybody who has been involved since 1854 is obviously not feasible, so let's start with four very special acknowledgements.

The first acknowledgment is to Marion Lucas who will serve as President of the International Association of Fairs and Expositions for the year 2001. During his tenure as Secretary/Manager of the Iowa State Fair and through his vision, the Blue Ribbon Foundation was created.

The second acknowledgement is to Dr. Chris Allen Rasmussen. His dissertation, *State Fair: Culture and Agriculture in Iowa, 1854-1941*, was written for Rutgers: The State University of New Jersey in New Brunswick in 1992. The information he gathered enabled us to share with you a richer history of the people and events that comprised much of the Fair's first 87 years.

The third acknowledgement is to you, the person holding this book. We thank you for your association with the Iowa State Fair, and we hope that time spent reading this story and looking at these marvelous photographs will serve to repay you for your support of an Iowa treasure.

The fourth acknowledgement is to Madelyn Levitt, another Iowa treasure. Her love for the Fair and her belief that its story was worthy of being told have helped make *Our State Fair Iowa's Blue Ribbon Story* a reality.

We are grateful to certain of you who worked diligently to take the project forward, or have been special friends of the Iowa State Fair. We list some names here. Others appear within the story itself. Thanks to:

Craig Agan, National Sprint Car Museum Hall of Fame; Joy Brace, Superintendent of Creative Arts; Mary Boysen, Superintendent of the Agriculture Building; Kevin Carpenter, Iowa FFA; Don Clark, former Superintendent of Horses and Ponies; The Honorable Ron Corbett, former Speaker of the Iowa House of Representatives; Art and Jeri Corey, whose early memories led to a life-long love for the Fair; Jerry Coughlon, former Competitive Events Director; Jennings Crawford, whose father kept the Fairgrounds lit; Floyd and Helen Deets, who have made the Fair part of their lives; Pamela Deitrick and Peter Bowers and all those in the research department of the Public Library of Des Moines; The Des Moines Register, with special thanks to Diane Graham, Cheri Sommers, Aric West and Jeff Zeleney; Mark Fischer, Iowa Agriculture and Land Stewardship Department; Eric Fogg, railroad enthusiast; C.J. Gauger, Chuck Morris and Denise Schwab, Iowa Youth and 4-H Program; The Gazette Company, Cedar Rapids, Iowa; Kay Gesaman, Superintendent of the Cultural Center; Dennis Goodwin, Promoter of Tractor and Truck Pull; Ross Harrison, Iowa Department of Natural Resources; Suzanne Hegarty and Joyce Hoppes, The Iowa Pork Producers Association; Frank Holdmeyer, Wallaces Farmer; Don Hummel, Superintendent of Sheep; Charles R. Hurburgh Jr. and Don Voelker, Iowa State University; The Late Emil Husak, State Senator; The Iowa Egg Council; The Iowa State Fair Staff; Gretta Irwin, The Iowa Turkey Federation; Daryl Jahn, Iowa Farm Bureau Federation; The Honorable JoAnn Johnson, State Senator; Dale Juergens, Clearfield Lions Club; Dr. Arlin Karsten, Kirkwood Community College; Jack Ketterer, Iowa Racing and Gaming Commission; Marjorie Lankford, Iowa State Fair Museum; Gene Maahs, Living History Farms; Rhonda Martin, Bob Lenc Landscaping, Inc., & Lawn Care; Bill McNarney; who contributed his artistic talent for renovation fundraising; George Mills, Iowa historian; Karen S. Moll, State Library of Iowa; John Mortimer, Beef Promotions of Iowa; Jim Murphy, Mighty Bluegrass Shows; Wayne Nattress, The Iowa FFA Foundation; Alan O'Neal, Iowa Department of Education; Jerry Parkin, whose continuous support for the Fair brings about results; Michael Pinckney, who grew up around the Fair; State Historical Society of Iowa - Des Moines, with special thanks to Gordon Hendrickson, Michael Smith and Ellen Westhafer; Mike Thompson; who shared his love of Fair history through research; Bill Turner, Superintendent of Horticulture; Earl Wagner, Champion Sprint Car driver and racing enthusiast; Steve & Linda Weldon, The Iowa Foundation for Agricultural Advancement; Dee Wolfe, Superintendent of Woodcarving; 75th, 76th, 77th, and 78th Iowa General Assemblies; and finally to Amy Houston for her coordination, dedication, persistence and extraordinary efforts in bringing this book to fruition.

A NOTE ABOUT THE PHOTOS

Designing this book was a rich experience for us because of the amazing photos we worked with. Some of the photographers are living and working now. Many are long gone. Most are unknown to us. All enriched our lives and made this book possible.

Most photos and posters come from the Iowa State Historical Society Archives section on the Iowa State Fair and from the Iowa State Fair Museum. Most objects come from the Iowa State Fair Museum. On page 270 there is more detailed information about photo credits. We thank all those who helped us find the visual images for this book.

Although most people in these photos are nameless, they have given us a real gift of a moment of their time at the Fair. We look into their eyes, we see them walking the same ground we walk every August and we know why the title of this book is *Our* State Fair.   -Paul Micich

Library of Congress Cataloging-in-Publication Data
Shanley, Mary Kay.
  Our state fair : Iowa's blue ribbon story / Mary Kay Shanley,
author.-- 1st ed.
    p. cm.
  ISBN 1-888223-17-0 (hardcover)
S555.I8 S53 2000
630'.74777--dc21
                              00-009331
Printed in the United States

AUTHOR
MARY KAY SHANLEY

RESEARCHER
WILLIAM CAMPFIELD

EDITOR
JULIA JOHNSTON

COPY EDITOR
DIANE DORO

ART DIRECTOR
PAUL MICICH

DESIGNERS
PAUL MICICH
LARASSA KABEL
MOLLY SPAIN
KATHERINE ZEPH

PHOTO RESEARCHER
ELLEN HAMMOND

PUBLISHER
IOWA STATE FAIR
BLUE RIBBON
FOUNDATION

PRINTER
SIGLER PRINTING &
PUBLISHING, AMES, IOWA

**IOWA STATE FAIR
BLUE RIBBON
FOUNDATION STAFF**

EXECUTIVE DIRECTOR
JOHN PUTNEY

ASSISTANT DIRECTOR
AMY HOUSTON

**SPONSORSHIP
DIRECTOR**
PAM BROCKER

**SPECIAL PROGRAMS
MANAGER**
ROBIN LAGE

FORMER STAFF
BETH (REINIG) GREINER
JOSETTE SCHIRA
EMILY (REIS) ABBAS

It Belongs To Us All

The Iowa State Fair is truly one of Iowa's greatest treasures. It is a vibrant, living legend that is immense in its scope and resilience. No other event is as venerable to Iowans or has stood the test of time better. It preceded the presidency of Abraham Lincoln. It has endured our nation's war involvement. It has survived politics, weather and economic hardships.

As we begin the new millennium and approach the 150th anniversary of the Iowa State Fair, we can reflect on the evolution of the Fair into what it is today. It is a time to recognize the efforts, creativity and tenacity of those who came before us. In doing so, perhaps we will gain an insight and appreciation for this wonderful legacy, its complexities and its value to past, present and future Iowa generations.

The Iowa State Fair is and always has been an important vehicle for economic development, education, tourism and recreation. It provides a means for showcasing the talents and abilities of both individuals and businesses. It brings Iowa's people together in a spirit of cooperation, competition, compassion and camaraderie. It is a seed from which immeasurable economic impact grows.

Yet it is more, for it is an institution that fulfills dreams, captures the imagination and bolsters the morale in young and old alike. It is an extremely important part of Iowa's heritage and culture—and it belongs to us all.

John Putney
Iowa State Fair Blue Ribbon Foundation

Contents

146
THE AG EXTRAVAGANZA OF IOWA

"Most of the farmers who come to the Fair come there because they don't intend to get left behind. They want to know the last word in up-to-date machinery and improved livestock, but they expect to get their best information from their fellow farmers whom they meet at the Fair."

196
THOSE SUPER STRUCTURES

"The complex contains a representative collection of almost all architectural styles for most of the past 200 years...[and] each of the architects involved respected the designs of those preceding architects."

218
MEET YOU AT THE FAIR

"Driving alone in time as their forefathers had driven in the space of the Iowa prairies, they felt a faint sense of adventure and the large sehnsucht [yearning]of a starry, slightly humid Iowa night."

ADMISSION TICKETS
·· HERE ··
ADULTS 35¢
CHILDREN 10¢

Our State Fair...
What's Good for America...

How best to describe the Iowa State Fair, an 11-day August institution which for nearly a million of us is a yearly super-special event? Actually, "State Fair" might be a misnomer. Because it really is "the people's fair." Our fair.

This is no easy assignment, not even for a newspaper farm editor who during his 33 years working for *The Des Moines Register and Tribune* spent the equivalent of an entire work year on the fairgrounds doing his thing - covering the Fair.

It is difficult to describe in brief what constitutes our State Fair. So I did some research on how others saw our Fair:

"The Iowa State Fair is a living museum which renews itself every August," proclaimed *Vacationland, U.S.A.* magazine nearly 30 years ago. It's "as wholesome as home-baked bread" added the late Iowa author/poet Paul Engle.

Bill Robbins of *The New York Times* in 1979 reported: "Nothing that happens in the nation's

heartland each summer is as big as the Iowa State Fair...it's an extravaganza of prized pigs, lambs and cattle...and blue ribbons...."

More recently, in *National Geographic Traveler* magazine, Pulitzer Prize-winning editor Michael Gartner called it "a long stroll into the past and a peek into the future."

In 1998 *The Des Moines Register* described the Iowa State Fair as "a place where know-how is on display—one of the final repositories of people who know how to do things..."

But one of the best descriptions we've heard came from *Successful Farming*. In 1999 writer/farmer and veteran Fair camper Bill Eftink called the Iowa State Fair "America's largest summer party...a quiet celebration of what's good for America."

To me, the Fair is sort of like a marvelous malady, a peculiar "ailment" which directly afflicts about a million people annually. It's a wonderful

kind of likeable, infectious "virus" you might call "State Fair Fever," which attacks yearly and can spread and infect whole families, and people of all ages and interests.

But mostly, the Fair is a place of memories. As a farm boy growing up in the 1930s, I recall how we —like countless others—did our milking long before daybreak in order to go to the Fair from our northern Iowa farm. And we never left to return home until after the fireworks. Years later, I remember how our three sons often protested to their mother how they only got to go to the Fair once or twice a year while "lucky Dad" got to go every day.

There were some rare days when you could become a part of the Fair. Like competing in what was then the all-male Cookout King Contest. My entry was a lamb-chop-grilling recipe provided by my wife Joann. I won—not because I was such a good cook, but because I was the only lamb-cooking entry!

There were other contests, too. Like the "celebrity" cow-milking contest where my milk-mate one year was a female television anchor (I wisely advised that she remove her huge turquoise ring before coming to grips with the Holstein cow's private parts). I won one year because my milking partner was a dairy princess who obviously knew her way around a milking parlor. Plus, our milk cow was a well-endowed (and un-milked) Brown Swiss. Another time we lost because the Milking Shorthorn cow, to the amusement of the Pavilion crowd, somehow slammed a hoof into our bucket, spilling its meager contents.

My personal State Fair highlight came in 1988 in the Governor's Charity Steer Show when *The Register* entered "Hot News," a muscular animal raised by Mark Putney of Gladbrook. I'll never forget the excitement I felt when judge Gene Wiese of Manning picked our steer champion.

Covering the Fair meant I could visit with dozens of people from virtually every county. This gave me a good statewide grassroots feel for what was going on in rural Iowa, like what crop prospects were, or if there was any matter of concern.

All in all, covering the Fair for more than three decades for my newspaper provided a special vantage point not given to many. Truly, it was an honor to be a part of what so many of us regard as the greatest State Fair in the world. And after all, our Fair is the composite of generations past, blended and shaped by us but kind of mixed in with the promise and our hopes for the Iowa of tomorrow. It's all there. Just like it has been for almost 150 years now—something good for our state, our country, and us all.

- Don Muhm

IOWA'S GREAT STATE FAIR

A GRAND TRADITION

THE FIRST FAIR AIRSHIP This forerunner of the blimp was the beginning of the aviation attractions.

ONE OF THE SPACIOUS rest porches of the Women and Children's building on the fair grounds.

8-24-1920

RUTH LAW, world famous woman aviator. The upper picture shows how her daring stunts in her illuminated plane appear at night.

BEACH MODELS, one of the diving acts that will be on the great midway. The members of the company have been drawn from the big film companies in California.

BY R.GELATT

LIEUT. K. W. THOM, director of the army exposition at the fair.

"Shall the resources of other States be developed, their wealth increased and their people elevated in the scale of intellectual being, and ours stand still?"

An invitation to join the Iowa State Agricultural Society, 1853

SEE THE AIRSHIP.

IOWA STATE FAIR,

DES MOINES,

AUGUST 24-31,

1906.

Let's just say that if Thomas Clagett from Keokuk and J.M. Shaffer from Fairfield came to our Iowa State Fair today, they would be—well—overwhelmed. Maybe even astounded. Probably flabbergasted. And, most likely, thunderstruck! That's because what they'd see today has precious little in common with the vision of a state fair those two entertained back in the mid-nineteenth century. Still, you really ought to know a bit about their vision because everything must start somewhere, and our Iowa State Fair started with them.

IOWA STATE FAIR

DES MOINES,
August 21---29,
1903.

On The Way to the Iowa State Fair
with Her Mortgage Lifter.

W. W. MORROW, President

J. C. SIMPSON, Secretar

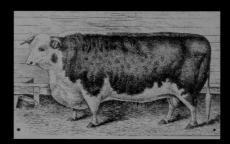

Back in 1853—seven years after Iowa became a state—we find Judge Clagett and Dr. Shaffer as busy members of the Jefferson County Agricultural Society. Curiously, neither they—nor perhaps any other members of the Agricultural Society—were actually farmers. Rather, they were businessmen, a point you'll want to remember later on.

Most counties by this time had ag societies. In fact, every free state in the Union except Iowa even had a state organization. Consequently, the Jefferson County Agricultural Society invited Iowa's other county societies to meet in Fairfield three days after Christmas of 1853 to form the Iowa State Agricultural Society (ISAS). As the invitation pointedly asked:

"Is it not time for the farmers of Iowa to be aroused to the importance of such an organization in this State? Shall the resources of other States be developed, their wealth increased and their people elevated in the scale of intellectual being, and ours stand still?"

Stern words, obviously, but even so, representatives from only five counties showed up for the meeting. Judge Clagett, not being there, was elected president. Dr. Shaffer became its first secretary. The ISAS's charge: to sponsor agricultural fairs—grand events where farmers, as well as manufacturers and homemakers, would bring together their products in "amicable rivalry." The Society believed the competition would educate the competitors, help-ing them improve their products. And quality products, eventually, would elevate Iowa to national prominence.

A QUICK HISTORY LESSON

The Old World market fair, which provided an opportunity for trade in the Middle Ages, still survives in some parts of Europe. Our agricultural fair, on the other hand, is relatively new and peculiarly American. Originally modeled after the English cattle show, the American fair is a combination of exhibit, instruction and amusement. Elkanah Watson, the father of our agricultural fairs, established the Berkshire Society that conducted cattle shows as far west as Ohio between 1849 and 1853. (In those days, Ohio was west.)

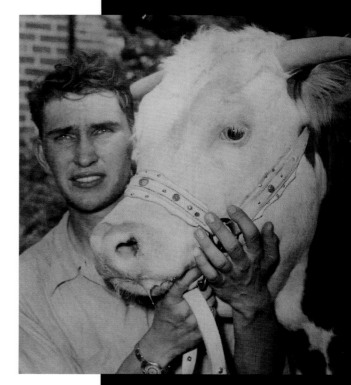

ONE ADMISSION

The ISAS's very first agricultural fair—the Iowa State Fair—was set for a Wednesday, Thursday and Friday in October 1854 in Fairfield. Oh, my, but that Fair was serious business, revolving around education, economics and cultural progress.

That first Fair was humble, too, if not meager. The fairgrounds covered six acres, surrounded by a high rail fence. Temporary sheds and pens housed livestock; a tent sheltered exhibits; and workers prepared a 1,500-foot horse track. It cost 25 cents per day to get in; the ISAS members and their families—except males over 21—were free.

There was no Midway or Varied Industries Building. You didn't eat corn dogs or funnel cakes. You couldn't bounce to the music of fiddle contestants, cheer on drivers in the auto races, tour Grandfather's Barn or watch buckskinners cook supper at their Rendezvous Encampment. Your children wouldn't spend hours grooming calves or tap dancing on the Bill Riley Stage. And nobody marveled at either a big boar or a butter cow.

Instead, you would have heard an hours-long address by an ISAS official; observed the judging of livestock, crops, fruits and vegetables; looked at prison-made agricultural implements; checked out Atkin's Self Raker and Reaper, as well as plows and corn planters so new they weren't yet on the market. And, of course, you would have viewed articles which Iowa ladies created from the loom, needle or pencil—articles of such quality that our women could be placed in opposition to "all the world and the rest of mankind" for their products.

But would you have had any fun? Well, it might have been fun to see Lee County admirers present Governor Grimes with a 360-pound chunk of Denmark cheese. You may have enjoyed watching a dog win the dog-and-bear fight, or women competing in equestrian events. But, by and large, having fun was not a goal. The Fair was a scientific exhibition, dedicated to the introduction of improved agricultural techniques and purebred livestock. The fun part was yet to come.

On with the Fairs!

In the beginning, nobody thought about where the State Fair would actually be held from one year to the next year. Consequently, the "Fair on Wheels" rolled around eastern Iowa from 1854 until 1879. First this county, then that one busily built or refurbished structures in hopes of getting the ISAS nod to host the upcoming Fair. Such constant moving around wasn't very practical, as the ISAS acknowledged in a report: "The fair is…arranged, organized, completed and dissipated in a week. Then the halls and stalls and buildings are left to decay with weeds and neglect for another year when the same process is repeated."

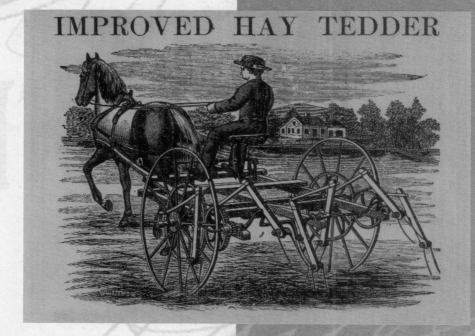

IMPROVED HAY TEDDER

Often, those counties who did host the Fair went back to the Society once the event was over, requesting reimbursement for expenses. But such pleas fell on deaf ears since the Society itself was always trying to break even. Some years, if you combined all of the gate receipts, local business donations, legislative appropriations, concession fees and ISAS dues, there still wasn't enough money to pay all the premiums awarded in competition.

Considering the money problems never went away, you have to wonder at some ISAS decisions. For example, the Fair was held in Keokuk in 1869 and 1870. Because of Keokuk's extreme south-eastern location, lots of Iowans stayed home, plunging the exposition into debt. Consequently, in 1871 the ISAS moved the Fair to Cedar Rapids, a fairly central location back then. After three years in Cedar Rapids, the ISAS was up $8,000, so the Society moved the Fair back to Keokuk (which, of course, was still in that extreme southeastern location).

This move did not find favor with *The Cedar Rapids Times*, which reported it wouldn't object to the Fair being in Keokuk if Keokuk "would accommodate anything like a fair share of the state." In fact, one year in Keokuk, the secretary received more requests for premium lists from Illinois and Missouri than from Iowa, causing folks to refer to the exposition as the "Illinois State Fair." (continued on page 22)

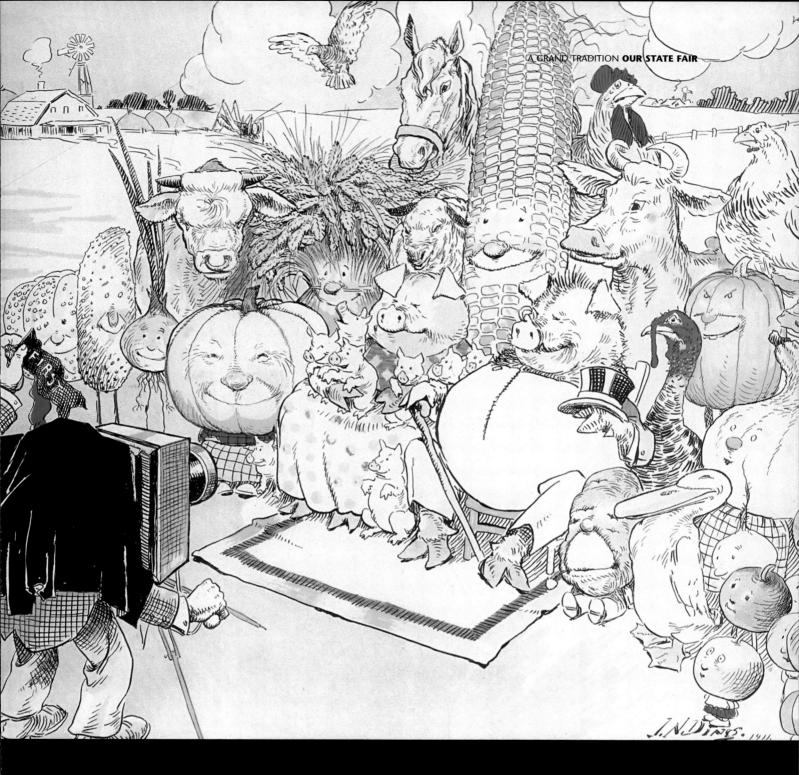

J.N.DING. 1911.

THE POLITICS OF IT ALL

In the beginning, the Legislature appropriated about $2,000 a year to the Fair—with no strings attached. Members of the Iowa State Agricultural Society, who ran the Fair, considered that to be a "good, round sum." But in 1874, when the Fair turned 20, it seemed that just about every public institution came begging the Legislature for money to improve this or enlarge that. According to the ISAS records, "Every one of these received at the hands of a liberal legislature nearly what they asked."

Unfortunately, that same year somebody discovered the Society had $8,000 in U.S. bonds. Consequently, the Legislature cut off funding to the Society. Well, the Society responded the way any normal group would: by urging voters to only elect candidates who supported continued state aid to the ISAS.

Eventually, funding resumed—but we don't know if that was connected to any candidate endorsements!

1892 Iowa State Fair 1892

ASSISTANT'S TICKET.

NOT GOOD IF TRANSFERRED TO ANY OTHER PERSON.

Good only for WEDNESDAY, AUGUST 31st, 1892.

UP TO 10 O'CLOCK A.M.

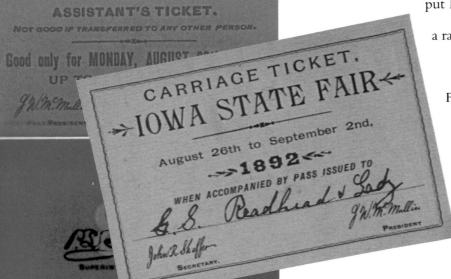

ASSISTANT'S TICKET.

NOT GOOD IF TRANSFERRED TO ANY OTHER PERSON.

Good only for MONDAY, AUGUST

UP TO

CARRIAGE TICKET.
→ IOWA STATE FAIR ←
August 26th to September 2nd,
→ 1892 ←
WHEN ACCOMPANIED BY PASS ISSUED TO

G. S. Readhead & Lady

J. W. McMullin
PRESIDENT.

John R. Shaffer
SECRETARY.

1892 Iowa State Fair 1892

REFRESHMENT TICKET.

NOT GOOD IF TRANSFERRED TO ANY OTHER PERSON.

Good only for THURSDAY, SEPTEMBER 1st, 1892.

UP TO 10 O'CLOCK A.M.

J. W. McMullin
PRESIDENT.

John R. Shaffer
SECRETARY.

Finally, in 1879, the ISAS decided to hold the Fair in Des Moines. The Society based its choice on continuing financial problems, a growing population in the central and western portions of Iowa (which put Des Moines pretty much in the middle), and a railroad system that connected the whole state. Railroads, in fact, had been part of the State Fair almost from the beginning—that being 1855, when rails bridged the Mississippi River at Rock Island. Twelve years later, in 1867, the Cedar Rapids and Missouri River Railroad Line reached Council Bluffs. Eventually, that city was designated as the eastern terminus for the Union Pacific, which extended across the western half of the country to Sacramento, California.

As those mighty black  steam-driven engines chugged their way across Iowa in the early days, railroad company executives quickly figured out that railroads could—indeed, should—be a part of the Fair. Most families had

Iowa State Fair 1892

ASSISTANT'S TICKET.

GOOD IF TRANSFERRED TO ANY OTHER PERSON.

Good only for MONDAY, AUGUST 29th, 1892.

UP TO 10 O'CLOCK A. M.

PRESIDENT.   SECRETARY.

been traveling to the Fair via covered wagon, with frontiersmen carrying long pistols in their belts for protection and decoration. The prospect of poor roads and unpredictable weather made the train infinitely more appealing. One year after the railroad arrived in Iowa, tracks were extended to Muscatine for the 1856 State Fair, which hosted between 10,000 and 15,000 fairgoers.

WAVING FLAGS AND BUNTING | Many Other Gorgeous and Marvelous Scenes

BUSINESS HOUSES DECORATED AS NEVER BEFORE | EVERY ★ RAILROAD ★ LEADS ★ TO ★ DES ★ MOINES

Entire Change of Program each Evening

HALF ★ FARE ★ WILL ★ BE ★ GIVEN ★ ON ★ THE ★ RAILROADS

r 1892

REFRESHMENT TICKET.

NOT GOOD IF TRANSFERRED TO ANY OTHER PERSON.

Good only for THURSDAY, SEPTEMBER 1st, 1892.

UP TO 10 O'CLOCK A. M.

PRESIDENT.   SECRETARY.

Such an attendance figure would stretch just about any city's housing accommodations in those days. To be helpful, the ISAS published the Muscatine hotel rates ahead of time. Every hotel except one conformed to those rates, that one charging a dollar per straw bed. This breach of promise made the ISAS mad—and we bet the guests weren't very pleased either!

After Muscatine, the railroads followed the Fair around, transporting people as well as freight to whichever city happened to be hosting the Fair. The railroads' efforts were appreciated. According to an 1856 editorial in *The Iowa City Republican*:

"The railroad facilities added very materially to the comfort, convenience and economy of visitors. Had it not been for the completion of this road, all the public conveyances in half a dozen such cities could not have carried the crowd when they wanted to be carried; and besides this, hacks would have charged fifty cents a trip, while the railroads charged twenty-five. It is doubtless time that the railroad could have made money and charged a still lower fare (which we hope it will do next year), but we should not condemn that which saves us half our money because it does not save all of it."

By the time the Fair opened in Des Moines—on August 30, 1879, to be exact—fairgoers could ride right up to the 60-acre fairgrounds on the Rock Island Railroad's spur line, laid especially for the Fair's eight-day run. The grounds were just west of the capital city in Brown's Park, bordered by Thirty-eighth and Forty-second Streets and by Center Street and Grand Avenue (then known as Greenwood Avenue). While the move to Des Moines probably was not intended to be permanent, the State Fair would never again grace another city.

As was typical, a high board fence surrounded the Des Moines fairgrounds. New, albeit temporary, construction included five large halls, offices for the Fair Board, judges' and reporters' stands, horse and cattle stalls, hog and sheep pens, a dining hall, an amphitheater and a racetrack. The campgrounds and most entertainment not related to farming were relegated to space outside the fence.

That first year, attendance swelled to more than 100,000 and net receipts totaled $28,000. Many Iowans had never visited the capital city and saw this as a holiday. By the next year, people within a 50-mile circuit who had come the first year merely to visit returned with the choicest of their products. And why not? Railroads were reducing passenger and freight rates and the press was pointing out excellence everywhere.

There's a train station in Heritage Village—at least we think it's a train station. Some speculate that it once served streetcar passengers traveling to and from the Fair. It's been around as long as anybody can remember and, since 1920, has stood east of Ye Old Mill. The little Pennsylvania Dutch-style building today is home to a collection of railroad memorabilia, photos and Railroad Express Agency equipment.

25

Railroads continued to play an important role in the State Fair through the end of the century. Some rail lines set up headquarters on the fairgrounds. Others sponsored "first-class cars, with fitting appointments, and placed under the direction of gentlemen who looked only to the safety and comfort of their patrons." One year, the Rock Island reported carrying nearly 140,000 people from the city to the Fair and back, in addition to 37,000 excursionists they picked up from points along the line. (The report proudly notes that not one of those persons received an injury.) The Chicago Burlington and Quincy distributed "emergency cars" at convenient points along their lines. But even then, almost every train reaching the city by midweek of the Fair had people standing in the aisles. And one year, when bad weather made the roads and the horse race-track so muddy that the ISAS tacked an extra day onto the Fair's run, the railroads extended their reduced fares, as well.

THE GREAT IOW

DES MOINES, IOWA,

VA STATE FAIR
EPT. 9 TO 18, 1897.

HOME AT LAST

By 1884, the Legislature had decided the Fair needed a permanent home for "development of agricultural, horticultural, stockraising and mechanical interests of the State." Entertainment still was not part of the Fair. (But if you got an ISAS official out behind the barn, he'd admit that proceeds from entertainment sure did help the bottom line.) The Legislature allocated $50,000 for the purchase of at least 200 but not more than 400 acres somewhere in Iowa. The "somewhere" was contingent upon a city matching the appropriation, which Des Moines did, thanks to Isaac Brandt, an eastside businessman.

Fair officials took possession of the land in June 1886. Then, as now, the "front door" was at East Thirtieth Street and Grand Avenue. By the time the Fair opened that September, 67 buildings had been constructed, in addition to a plethora of private booths, houses and sheds for food,

By the time the Fair opened that September, 67 buildings had been constructed...

refreshments, amusements and entertainment. One would think the economic stability of future Fairs was guaranteed.

Not so! Poor crops, bad weather and hard times affected attendance. Plus, a permanent home called for new construction as well as upkeep of buildings. All of this drained the Society's treasury, causing the ISAS to turn to the Legislature for increasing financial

assistance. That situation created curious bedfellows. On the one hand, there was the ISAS—a private corporation that regarded itself as the spokesperson for agricultural interests of Iowa. On the other hand, there was the Legislature—a government body partially funding the work of this private corporation with taxpayer monies. Plus the Legislature owned the fairgrounds! So, in reality, the ISAS was not a private corporation, but rather a quasi-government body dependent upon public assistance.

Then, too, there was the Iowa State College of Agriculture and Mechanic Arts. When the Ames land grant college opened in 1868, the ISAS took a paternal approach, even having its president appointed to the College Board of Directors. However, the college rapidly

Streets a Sea of Flame

THOUSANDS OF
ELECTRIC ★ AND ★ GAS ★ LIGHTS

THE HEAVENS ABLAZE

With SCREECHING, THUNDERING BOMBS, thrown from PONDEROUS MORTARS.

THE AIR FILLED WITH
ENTRANCING MUSIC
Given by Hundreds of Musicians.

GRANDEST PYROTECHNIC DISPLAY
EVER WITNESSED.

IOWA'S HISTORY
SYMBOLIZED ★ BY
Mammoth Moving Floats

gained prestige for its approach to agriculture, which was rooted in education and research—unlike the ISAS approach. Additionally, the ISAS-sponsored competition at each Fair was meant to inspire better farming practices. But the judges provided by the ISAS were not necessarily experts in the categories they were judging. In fact, sometimes the judges just happened to be people who were standing around with nothing to do when the competition started—a practice the college did not endorse.

...the ISAS pinned its hopes for a successful 1893 on Mt. Vesuvius.

As if there wasn't enough turmoil for the ISAS, the Society was forced to cancel the Fair in 1898. The story actually begins earlier than that—in the summer of 1893, when America was experiencing a financial panic and the World's Fair was in Chicago—close enough to compete with Des Moines. Those could have been reasons enough to cancel the 1893 State Fair. Instead, the ISAS pinned its hopes for a successful 1893 on Mt. Vesuvius.

For some time, Des Moines had been offering its own entertainment during the State Fair Week (continued on page 38)

SEE THE
Flock of
Aerial Crafts

Progress made in solving problem
of navigation of the Heavens

FIVE AIR SHIPS
TWO BALLOONS

AMONG THE DOMES
State House, Des Moines
During Fair of 1906
WHEN SEVEN SUCCESSFUL FLIGHTS
WERE MADE WITH
A KNABENSHUE'S
AIR
SHIP

EXCITING BALLOON RACES

KNABENSHUE'S PASSENGER AIR SHIP

FIRST AND ONLY APPEARANCE
IN IOWA OF THE
Largest Air Ship Ever Built in America

THREE PROPELLERS--TWO 10-H. P. ENGINES

Aeroplane Attachments, Capable of Carrying
Three People.

Daily Flights and Exhibitions

Iowa
State Fair and Exposition
August 26, 27, 28, 29, 30, '07

...e on the captive Balloon, securely anchored by 750 feet of tested cable.

Visiting Soldiers' Monument—Iowa State Fair, 1906

24

Grand Avenue, Des Moines

THANK YOU, ISAAC BRANDT!

You can't deny that Isaac Brandt led an interesting life! Not only was he an aggressive eastside merchant who shook enough money loose from Des Moines businessmen to keep the Iowa State Fair in town forever, but he also was a conspirator with John Brown, who led the ill-fated raid on Harper's Ferry, Virginia, two years before the start of the Civil War.

Mr. Brown had come through Iowa several times, heading to Canada with fugitive slaves hiding under cornstalks in a wagon. Occasionally, he would stop at Mr. Brandt's home.

In 1884, 25 years after Mr. Brown was hanged by Virginia authorities for the raid, the Iowa Legislature allocated $50,000 for the purchase of land to become a permanent home for the State Fair. The host city would have to come up with matching funds. Determined that the fairgrounds be in or near Des Moines, Mr. Brandt began a personal campaign, raising $55,000 in pledges, on which he collected $51,000. Some of the funds came from the railroads that were, by this time, carrying tens of thousands of people to and from the exposition every year.

With money in hand, the Legislature purchased 266 acres at $175 per acre and three acres at $1,000 per acre from Calvin Thornton, a cabinet-maker and farmer who had come to Polk County almost 40 years earlier. Mr. Brandt stood at the highest spot on the land, situated about two miles east of the State Capitol, and deemed it "Inspiration Point." He suggested that a boulevard lead from the new fairgrounds into the city and that it be called Grand Avenue. Today, Mr. Brandt's Grand Avenue runs to the western edge of West Des Moines.

Two buildings from the Thornton farm remain—the home in which the Superintendent of Buildings and Grounds and his family live, and the old barn. It used to house the mules that worked at the Fair, as well as the superintendent's milk cow. Today, it is the beloved Grandfather's Barn. Opened to the public for the first time in 1973, the building is a classic example of the basement barn. The foundation is of native stone; walls are of hewn and rough Iowa lumber, meticulously mortised and tendoned together and secured with wrought iron nails. (They just don't build barns like that anymore!)

35

HERE'S WHAT HAPPENED AS ROCKET EXPLODED!

CHILDREN! COME TO MINE'S BIRTHDAY PARTY!

PICTORIAL SECTION

WALLACES' FARMER
Iowa AND Homestead

GOOD FARMING   CLEAR THINKING   RIGHT LIVING

16 PAGES OF PICTURES

DES MOINES, IOWA, AUGUST 15, 1936

IOWA PRESENTS HER GREATEST STATE FAIR

Gala Opening August 28th

Inspiration!

Education!

Thrills!

ALL ABO-O-O-ARD for Iowa's great summer vacation — the Iowa State Fair. In this section are a few scenes from the big outing the State Fair has prepared for over 350,000 Iowans this summer.

Above—THE RACE TRACK and grand stand where rodeo, horse races, auto races, hippodrome and thrill features will hold sway. Left—Part of the "Million Dollar" stock parade; Right —The baby health contest; Below —Chuck wagon racing, one of the new "thrill" features.

37

to promote the city. This particular year, Des Moines decided to host a fireworks re-enactment of the destruction of Pompeii. Believing anyone who came to Des Moines to see that spectacle would also come to the State Fair, the ISAS contributed $1,000 to bring the Pompeii show to town.

Well, folks did come to Des Moines to watch the fireworks, but they didn't stop by the Fair, and financially the ISAS took a drubbing. ISAS Secretary John Shaffer resigned, and it took the ISAS until 1897 to rebound financially. But as the '98 Fair discussions got underway, the familiar black cloud of competition reappeared—this time the Trans-Mississippi Exposition, which was to be in Omaha.

> *"...it appears that we had just as well go in the hole with a Fair as without."*

What to do? What to do? "Well," said Secretary P. L. Fowler, "when we consider that if we do not hold a Fair, we will go in the hole from $3,000 to $5,000, it appears that we had just as well go in the hole with a Fair as without."

Eventually the Board decided to hold the Fair if the good people of Des Moines would provide $5,000 in assistance. A meeting was called for April 13, 1898, at 11 A.M., at which time city representatives were to present the $5,000 to the ISAS. When no city representatives showed up at the meeting, the ISAS declared "that no Fair be held by the Iowa State Agricultural Society in the year 1898." Later, city representatives said nobody ever told them about the meeting—which was too bad because they had collected the $5,000.

In the end, however, none of that mattered anyway. One week later, Congress passed a resolution empowering President McKinley

Captured German canon shown at the 1920 Fair.

to use military force to drive Spanish armed forces from Cuba. Five days later, the U.S. declared war on Spain; that same day, the state began converting the fairgrounds into a military encampment.

Actually, the ISAS almost cancelled the Fair in 1861 too. The Civil War had begun that April, when troops fired on Fort Sumter, a U.S. military post in Charleston, South Carolina. The Fair was to begin on September 24, on the Johnson County Fairgrounds in Iowa City. Not surprisingly, many Iowans, as well as some members of the press and the ISAS, thought the Fair should be cancelled. In fact, that spring and summer, the fairgrounds had been transformed into

39

Camp Fremont, serving soldiers of the voluntary company. Those men didn't move out until September 21. And sure enough, three days later, the Fair opened.

The transformation from battlefield training ground to agriculture exposition was a real challenge, especially considering the destruction the soldiers had caused while camping there. Iowa could be grateful, however. Indiana, Wisconsin and Minnesota soldiers caused so much damage to their respective fairgrounds that their state fairs had to be cancelled that year.

Even without Camp Fremont, reminders of the war were everywhere. For example, First Iowa Volunteers patrolled the grounds during the four-day event. And whenever someone's name was called to bring forth his entry into competition and a friend responded with, "He is absent," it was understood that the person had gone to war.

Still, bad weather, not the war, was blamed for low attendance and the meager displays of grains and vegetables. In fact, once the exposition was over, the hometown *Iowa City Republican* observed that while all preceding Fairs had been successful, this one was, indeed, a failure. *The Davenport Democrat and News*, on the other hand, had predicted the Iowa City Fair would be a failure before it began. *The Iowa City Republican* said that was done to prevent persons in the eastern portion of the state from attending the Fair in the first place.

In the end, however, it was the ISAS that got cancelled for good. In 1902, the Legislature established the Department of Agriculture and charged the State Board of Agriculture with managing the Fair. Thus, the ISAS was legislated out of existence. Twenty-one years later, the Legislature created the State Fair Board, which has been responsible for the Fair ever since.

UPS AND DOWNS—BUT MOSTLY UPS

As good as it was, the Fair experienced a couple of major bumps in the road—first with The Great Depression in the '30s and then with the cancellation of the Fair from 1942–1945 because of World War II.

Already in 1941, patriotism was playing a highly visible role at the Fair. A "Victory" arch spanned the main entrance with a replica of the Statue of Liberty surmounting the center of the arch, flanked by murals depicting the joint task of agriculture and industry in strengthening the defense of the nation. Main buildings sported patriotic banners and flags; the Army, Navy and Marine Corps demonstrated everything from machine guns to jeeps, trench mortars and rapid-fire rifles; the Farm Bureau, poultry industry and meat producers highlighted the farmers' part in strengthening America's efforts.

Still, when the Fair wrapped up on Friday, August 29, 1941, nobody had a clue that the event would be cancelled the next year— not to mention 1943, 1944 and 1945. As a matter of fact, the board was busily planning the 1942 exposition when the Axis powers declared war on the United States on December 11, 1941. The board debated whether it would be appropriate to continue with its plans, then decided in favor—using the Fair as a way to appeal to farmers to produce more livestock and food products.

But those plans, patriotic as they were, got shelved in the Spring of '42 when the U.S. Army Air Corps requested permission to turn the fireproof buildings on the fairgrounds into storage depots. The board said yes, charging the military $1 per year. That left only the Grandstand, racetrack, horse barns, shops and storage buildings. Because you couldn't fit an Iowa State Fair into spaces that small, the board voted to hold a 4-H Club show and educational fair instead,

Dear Sir:

by the Iowa

recent sug

the Office

of Agricul

still emphasizing food production. Exhibits would be housed beneath the Grandstand and in tents east and north of the racetrack.

In the end, however, the government issued a formal appeal for cancellation of all larger fairs as a tire conservation measure, and the board acquiesced. Until the end of World War II, the Fair Board's sole job was to act as custodian for the grounds and buildings, making sure the property was properly cared for and working with military authorities.

Not surprisingly, there was no criticism leveled at the board for its decision. Rather, members were praised for their patriotism.

A common goal of both the State Board of Agriculture and the State Fair Board was and remains to offer something for every single fairgoer. Take a look, if you will, at a bit of what went on in just one decade— the 1920s:

In **1920**, the Cattle Barn—one of the largest in the country—was completed.

In **1921**, audiences crowded into the Women and Children's Building for lectures and demonstrations. Educational specialists and home economists went beyond traditional topics like cooking to share information about how Iowa's rural women could run a better home and build a better community. One visitor from Minnesota remarked that such crowds of eager listeners could not have been assembled at her state fair.

In **1922**, the National Horseshoe Tournament attracted 86 men and women from 13 states, including New York and California—attesting to the popularity of "barnyard golf." As noted in a Fair Board report, the game originally "was confined quite largely to farmers [but] the new game seems to be followed extensively by their city cousins." Of the 16 players in final competition, nine were Iowans, with Frank Lundin, 22, from New London, ringing his way to the national championship.

In **1923**, the new 4-H Club Dining Hall opened. That year, more than 9,200 meals were prepared for the Iowa Boys and Girls 4-H Club members at a cost of 30 cents per meal. The cooks did such a good job that there was "practically no sickness among club members."

In **1924**, a pedigreed dog show, recognized by the American Kennel Club, attracted dog fanciers as well as folks who'd never seen a dog show in their whole lives.

In **1925**, the Iowa State Fair and Exposition became the Iowa State Fair and National Livestock Show, drawing attention to the scope of livestock entries.

In **1926**, "The Birth of the Messiah" opera featured Arthur Middleton, an Iowa native and leading baritone of the Metropolitan Opera Company. The production attracted 4,500 people to the Grandstand, plaza seats and bleachers. While deemed a success, people agreed the surroundings weren't as conducive to opera as, perhaps, to horse racing and fireworks.

In **1927**, Captain Charles Lindbergh circled the fairgrounds and racetrack at a low altitude several times in his "Spirit of St. Louis." That same year, Iowa native Clarence D. Chamberlin, later the first pilot to carry a passenger across the Atlantic, was an honored guest.

In **1928**, the Modern Woodmen of America camped near the streetcar entrance. The 30 drill teams competed and presented a series of military formations.

In **1929**, the Fair's Diamond Jubilee featured a Fairfield Chamber of Commerce exhibit recalling the first Iowa State Fair.

How's that for a little variety!

A *Des Moines Register* editorial pointed out the Iowa State Fair wasn't the only one affected by the war:

> We saw the other day a story of another fair that was interrupted by the war. Its history goes clear back to 1213, when King John of England granted a charter to Amersham's Whit-Monday cattle market and fair. The charter provided that it should lapse if the fair were not held each year. So during the last few years, John Robarts of Shenley had annually led an animal to Amersham for the Whit-Monday Sale, and John Cope of Homer Green had annually been the buyer. This year, neither could be present, so at last Amersham's 729-year-old fair had lapsed.
>
> But not the Iowa State Fair. Oh, no! Come peace, it will flower again, no doubt in greater glory than ever.

Indeed, 514,036 people flocked to the 1946 Fair to celebrate Iowa's first 100 years as a state. It was the first time attendance had exceeded the half-million mark. Then in 1954, the Fair celebrated its own centennial with a visit from President Dwight D. Eisenhower and Iowa native and former President Herbert Hoover. Earlier, officials had announced that nobody got into the Fair that year without paying their 50 cents. So Ike took officials at their word, handing over a dollar for himself and Mr. Hoover. That embarrassed Governor William Beardsley but apparently not Fair Secretary Lloyd Cunningham, who claimed to have placed the President's dollar in a vault of mementos to be opened in 2054. (continued on page 46)

"Considering the number of cars on the ground and the careless abandon displayed by those pedestrians who habitually walk one way and look another, one is astonished at the small number of accidents."

Department of Agriculture Fair Report, 1913

A CASE FOR CARS

About the time the ISAS was being replaced by the State Board of Agriculture, trains were giving way to streetcars. By 1905, the Des Moines Streetcar Company was moving between 100,000 and 200,000 people a year. (You're right—there's a big difference between 100,000 and 200,000, but that's how the Department of Agriculture report reads.) Out-of-towners could stay either in a local hotel or apply to the Commercial Club for accommodations. Railroads became less apt to offer reduced fares or maintain regular schedules, and railroad officials grumbled that they weren't making a profit.

And then, of course, there were all those automobiles bumping on down the road. By 1913, Iowans owned 71,000 cars, and so many of them showed up at the Fair that "storing" them became a problem. Cars filled the streets and were parked in every available open space, including the grounds. Fair management realized that either the city would have to widen the streets so cars could park on both

sides, or more fairgrounds space would have to be devoted to parking.

By 1915, car registration in Iowa was at 145,000—and an unofficial count determined that 20,000 people came to the Fair in automobiles. They drove in with camping outfits strapped on behind the car, plus baggage and lunchboxes piled atop the rumble seats, running boards and front fenders. The Fair Board determined that such a show of success must be the result of farming abundance.

The automobile exhibit on the first floor of the amphitheater that year consisted of 44 makes of cars—four through eight cylinders, roadsters, touring cars, coupes, electric drive and gasoline-propelled—plus 20 booths of accessories. The auto was becoming so popular so quickly that the next year, specialists connected with the engineering department at Iowa State College of Agriculture and Mechanic Arts in Ames presented daily lectures about the care and upkeep of the car. They figured

with Iowans spending $25 million a year on tires and accessories, those expenditures should be made wisely.

In 1972, 16 acres were purchased in the northeast corner of the fairgrounds, with access off University Avenue, for additional parking. Later still, land south of the fairgrounds, across Dean Avenue, was purchased from the Rock Island Railroad for overflow parking. Today, about one-fourth of the fairgrounds' 400 acres is designated for parking.

45

In 1951, the Fair's run was extended from eight to 10 days because of increasing attendance and a need for more time to show all the livestock, as well as a hedge against rainy weather. In 1976, the Fair grew to 12 days because of the Bicentennial. Almost every year since then, the Fair has been 11 days.

Also changed was the Fair's starting date. Typically, the fair ran during the last week of August and the first week of September.

THE WAY THEY'LL BE COMING TO THE STATE FAIR IN THE 'NEAR' FUTURE

But in the late '40s, school districts began inching their starting dates up into late August, which took its toll on Fair attendance. In response, the board kept moving its own starting date up until, finally, in 1983, the Fair opened earlier than ever—August 10. That year, 611,000 folks poured onto the fairgrounds. Not bad, considering the heat. (On Older Iowans Day, the temperature reached 106 degrees.)

In the last quarter of the 20th century, enticing folks to the Fair has been honed into a science. There are two-for-one admissions, free entertainment on the grounds day and night, advanced discounts on tickets, souvenirs for sale pretty much everywhere, a State Fair cookbook, Grandstand tickets available on a nationwide basis—the list goes on and on.

Souvenir
FAIR PROGRAM
IOWA STATE FAIRGROUNDS • 1951
ENABNIT
YOUR GUIDE TO
ENJOY THE FAIR
25¢
★ Places To See
★ Pictures and Maps
★ Daily Schedules

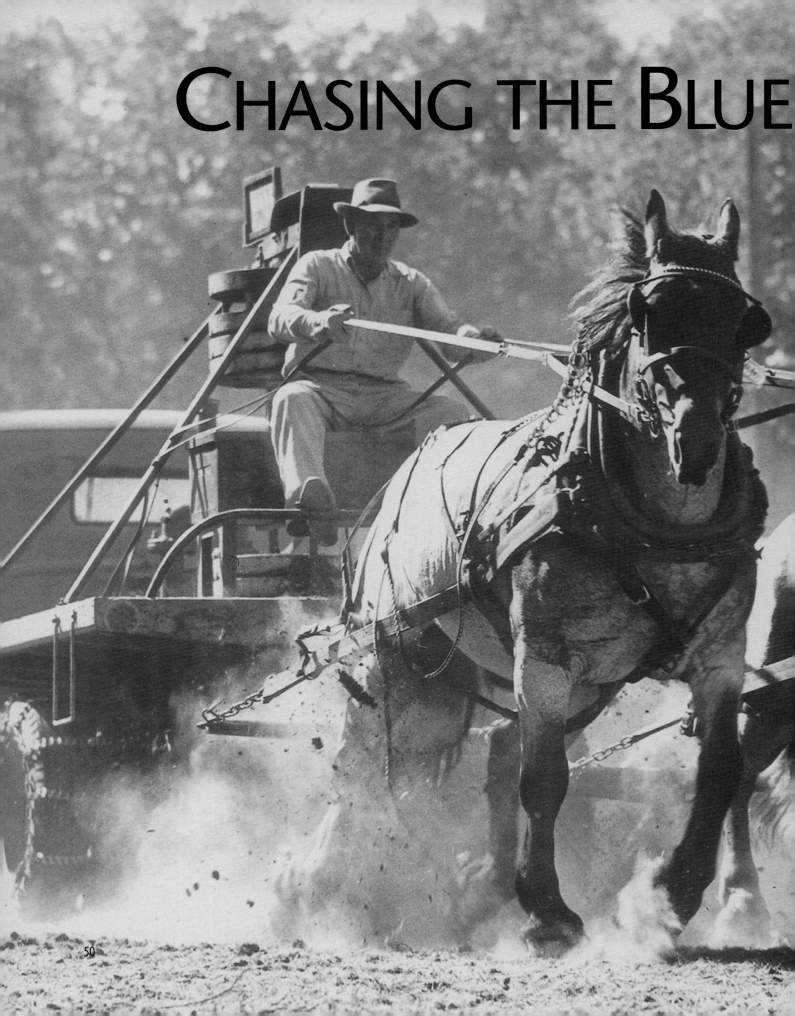

CHASING THE BLUE

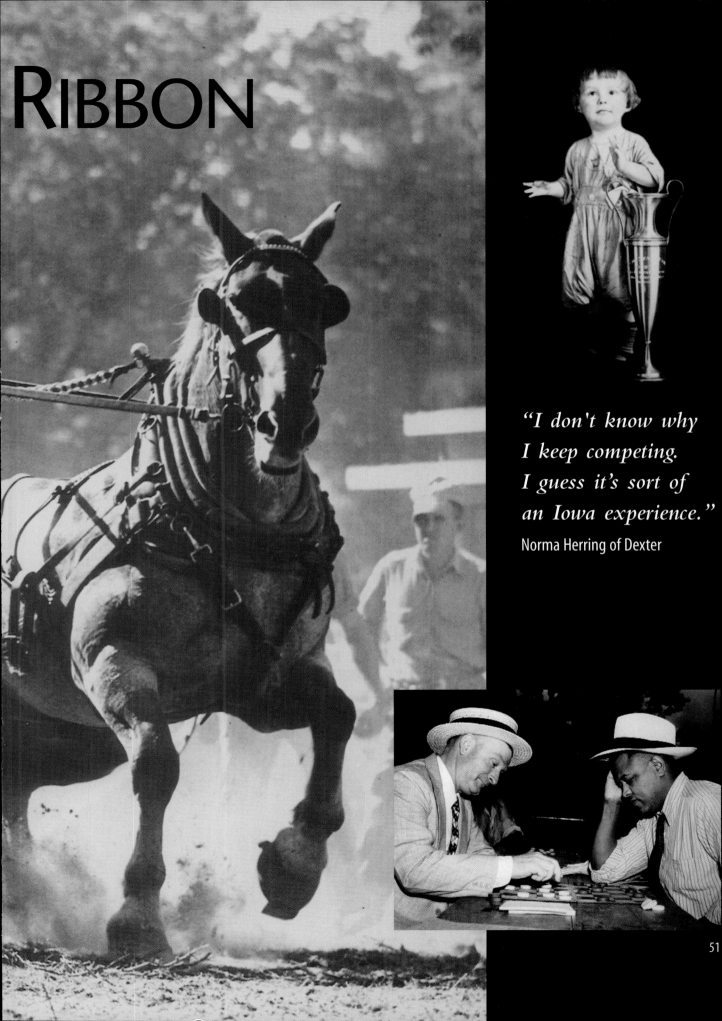

RIBBON

"*I don't know why
I keep competing.
I guess it's sort of
an Iowa experience.*"

Norma Herring of Dexter

51

Norma Herring's favorite contest is probably Spotlighting Spuds because her husband loves potatoes so much. Mrs. Herring puts potatoes in her cinnamon rolls, casseroles and soup. In fact, one year that soup won a blue ribbon at the Iowa State Fair. "It was a version of my mother's soup," Mrs. Herring confides. "I was thrilled because my mother passed away six years ago, and I'm sure she knew I was using her recipe."

Right this minute, however, the spotlight's on the Dexter woman's chili, not her potato soup. It's one of 18 entries in the 1999 Mrs. Grimes Chili Cook-Off Contest in Homemakers' Theater at the Maytag Family Center. Within the next hour, three judges seated at long tables in the front of the room will have looked at, sniffed and tasted lots of chili. The audience—chili cooks, family members, people who cook chili but never enter contests and people who've never seen food judged in their whole lives—watch quietly.

Competition and food are serious matters at the State Fair.

"I don't know why I keep competing," Mrs. Herring, 75, leans over and whispers. "I guess it's sort of an Iowa experience."

A judge is discussing the topping on one particular bowl of chili. "I don't put topping on my chili," she whispers again. "That changes the taste."

Norma Herring

52

53

When Norma Herring was a girl, her family didn't have much money, but they always came to the Iowa State Fair with a picnic lunch in tow. For the last 30 years, she's been a competitor with several hundred blue ribbons to show for it.

Mrs. Herring turns her attention back to the table at the front of the room. Some entries have been removed. "That means they won't win," Mrs. Herring comments. Spying hers still on the table, she sits forward, then leans back, hands folded in her lap. At long last, a judge stands up to announce the winners.

The fifth place winner is—

not Mrs. Herring.

The fourth place winner is—

not Mrs. Herring.

The third place winner is—

Mrs. Herring.

"Oh," she says, leaning forward again. "That's mine! I'm happy, but I'd have been happier with first place."

She sits back once more, waiting to hear the names of the first- and second-place winners whom, most likely, she'll know. But the judge has put down his microphone, interrupted by a minor amount of bustling down front. Eventually, he steps forward again to tell the audience that there was a mix-up in winners' names. So he starts over, announcing fifth place, then fourth, third and second place. With each announcement, the corresponding bowl of chili is moved off the table. Until there is only one entry left.

This time, the blue ribbon goes to Norma Herring.

"Oh," she says, leaning forward again. "That's mine! I'm happy, but I'd have been happier with first place."

FOOD, GLORIOUS FOOD!

Iowa State Fair Foods Superintendent Arlette Hollister has seen it all as far as food competition is concerned, and she can tell you everything about it.

Question: What state fair has the largest food competition?

Arlette: Ours, of course! In 1999, we awarded more than $50,000 in cash, bonds, gift certificates, books and food products. The total keeps getting bigger every year.

Q. How many categories of food competition do you offer?

A. We have 160 divisions and 863 classes. Pie is a division; cherry pie is a class.

Q. What categories receive the most and the least entries?

A. The most entries are cinnamon rolls, probably because Tone Bros., Inc., awards $3,000 to the first-place winner. Before cinnamon rolls, it was cakes. The fewest entries are buffalo because it's been difficult to purchase buffalo meat in Iowa.

Q. How does a new category come into existence?

A. Sometimes, I go to my cupboard and copy an 800 number off a box. Sometimes, a company spokesperson calls, asking to sponsor a competition. Once, the person in charge of

printing for the Iowa State Fair gave me a coupon he'd found at the grocery store. On the coupon, it said, "Call Debbie at 1-800..., which I did, and now Creamettes Pasta is a sponsor.

Q. What companies have been long-time sponsors and what category has been dropped?

A. Nestlé® ChocoBAKE®, Tone Bros., Inc., and Chiquita Brand, Inc., have been around forever. We dropped edible flowers because there were only two entries.

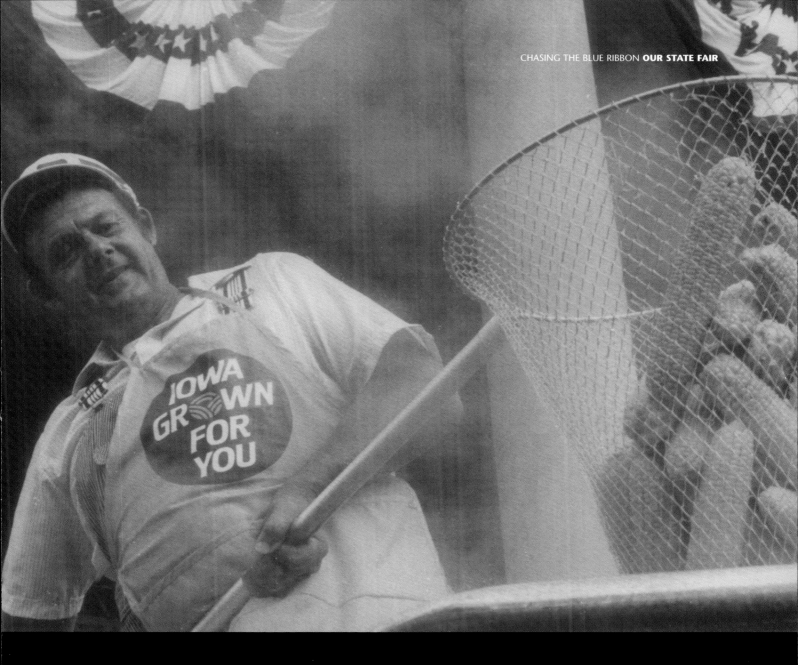

Q. Tell us a funny story about food competition?

A. Somebody brought in cornmeal muffins with bugs in them. I didn't know what to do, so I called the State Department of Health and was told there would be no problem because the bugs were baked. Then, we discovered the entry came from the Insectary Building within the Entomology Department at Iowa State University.

Q: Can you describe the contestants?

A: They're very imaginative. They like to try new things. More and more of them are men. And none of the contestants is a cutthroat competitor.

Q. What is the most unusual category?

A. One is the kids' Ugliest Cake competition; it can get really gross. After we got cakes with dead fish on them, we made a rule that an entry must be edible. One entry looked like a box of cat litter with Tootsie Rolls on top. Originally, the competition was also open to adults, but all they did was bring in cakes that had fallen. Another unusual category is the Mystery Sack competition. Each contestant gets a sack of groceries. Every sack has the same ingredients, but the ingredients don't necessarily go together. Like there might be tuna fish, baby food and anchovies. Each contestant can bring along three condiments. Then, they're given a spoon and a skillet, and they have 30 minutes to prepare something edible. One year, we put Fruit Roll.Ups in the bag, and the adult contestants couldn't figure out how to unroll them. So we had to get a little girl out of the audience to show them.

FOUR GENERATIONS OF GLORIOUS FOOD

This is a story about four women from Centerville. It speaks to how much things change and how much they remain the same. And in that respect, this is a story about all of us.

It begins with Mildred Phillips, who taught her daughter, Olive Jean Tarbell, to be a State Fair blue ribbon cook. Then, Olive Jean taught her daughter, Robin Tarbell-Thomas, to be a State Fair blue ribbon cook. Then, Robin taught her daughter, Molly Thomas, to be a State Fair blue ribbon cook. And since Molly's just 7, we can only assume the tradition will continue.

Actually, the story starts one generation earlier since Mildred learned to cook from her mother, Eva Horstman. Eva won festival and jamboree blue ribbons, but Mildred was the first in the family to bring home a State Fair blue ribbon.

We don't think Mildred, who died in 1992, would be surprised at her descendants' success. After all, the family has been cooking up winners for about 100 years. Still, she might find it both curious and comforting to know that these days Olive Jean, 68, and Robin, 39, are updating the recipes she and Eva used so many years ago.

Here, for your palatable pleasure, are four blue ribbon recipes from four Centerville women who are winners.

Olive Jean Tarbell's Penuche Candy

2 cups brown sugar
1 cup white sugar
3 tablespoons white syrup

1 cup thick cream
1 cup nutmeats
1 teaspoon vanilla

Mix the sugars, syrup and cream together. Cook until mixture forms a very soft ball (234°–238°) when dropped in cold water. Remove from stove. Let stand until mixture is cool, then beat until it begins to stiffen. Add the nuts and vanilla; pour into a buttered 8- by 8-inch pan; cut into squares.

Robin Tarbell-Thomas's Spice Drop Cookie Recipe

3/4 cup shortening
1/2 cup sugar
1/2 cup honey
1 egg

1/4 cup sorghum
1 banana, mashed
2 cups all-purpose flour
2 teaspoons baking soda

1/4 teaspoon salt
1 teaspoon ground cinnamon
1/2 teaspoon ground cloves
1/2 teaspoon ground ginger

Mix together shortening, sugar, honey, egg, sorghum and banana. Stir together flour, soda, salt and spices; stir into banana mixture. Drop by teaspoon onto ungreased baking sheets. Sprinkle with a cinnamon-sugar mixture, if desired. Bake in 350° oven about 8 minutes or until done.

Molly Thomas's Puppy Chow

1 stick margarine
1 cup peanut butter
12 oz milk chocolate chips

12 oz corn and rice Chex® cereals, mixed together
2 cups powdered sugar

Melt margarine and peanut butter together on low heat, stirring gently. Add milk chocolate chips, stirring until well blended. Add cereal to mixture. Pour into a brown paper bag. Add powdered sugar. Shake until well coated. Store in the refrigerator.

Mrs. Keith Phillips's Cake Donuts

2 eggs
1 cup sugar
2 teaspoons shortening, melted

3 cups flour
2 teaspoons baking powder
1/2 teaspoon salt
1/4 teaspoon ground cinnamon

1/4 teaspoon ground nutmeg
1 cup milk
1/2 teaspoon vanilla

Beat together eggs and sugar; stir in shortening. Sift together flour, baking powder, salt, cinnamon and nutmeg. Combine milk and vanilla. Add dry ingredients alternately with milk mixture, beating well after each addition. Roll out dough to 1/2 to 3/4 inch thickness; cut with doughnut cutter. Fry in deep hot fat (375°) until golden, about 1 minute per side. Drain.

COMPETING WAY BACK WHEN

We wonder if the Norma Herrings of the world made chili back in the 1850s when the Iowa State Agricultural Society began sponsoring its annual Fair. If so, that chili would have been entered in Household and Domestic Productions competition, ordinarily the category with the most entries. Next came Horses, then Cattle, and Agricultural and Horticultural Productions.

Only four of the 14 categories of competition were not directly related to agriculture. Surprised? Well, not if you know the Fair was created as a "scientific exhibition, dedicated to improving agricultural techniques and purebred livestock." Educating the farmer was so important that the society even sponsored an agricultural essay competition and conducted evening lectures. (The lecture at the Oskaloosa Congregational Church on opening night of the 1858 Fair concerned the "discussion in relation to field crops and kitchen vegetables.")

But what Iowans really liked was the competition, which the ISAS believed would spur them to improve their products to the point where their quality would gain national recognition. At first, runners-up winners received awards or premiums in the form of a silver plate, books, a membership in the ISAS (continued on page 64)

...the Fair was created as a "scientific exhibition, dedicated to improving agricultural techniques and purebred livestock."

Iowa State Fair, 1890

Class _____ Entry No _____

SECOND PREMIUM

This card must not be attached to any article that is not named in the Premium List. In such cases, where the article is worthy of a Premium, make your recommendation on Book.   JOHN R. SHAFFER, Secretary.

_____ Judge.

61

SEAL OF THE STATE OF IOWA

No 424

IOWA

Iowa State Fair, 1890

Class _____ Entry No _____

FIRST PREMIUM

This card must not be attached to any article that is not named in the Premium List. In such cases, where the article worthy of a Premium. make your recommendation on
JOHN R. SHAFFER. Secretary.

_____ Judge

State Fair, 189

Class _____ Entry No _____

THIRD PREMIUM

This card must not be attached to any article that is named in the Premium List. In such cases, where the article is worthy of a Premium. make your recommendation Book.
JOHN R. SHAFFER. Secretary

IOWA
STATE FAIR
AND
EXPOSITION
DES MOINES
1939
FIFTH PR
CATTLE DEPAR
IOWA GUER
SPECIAL

IOWA STATE FAIR
1949
GRAND CHAMPION
FARMERS & AMATEUR
HORSESHOE PITCHING
TOURNAMENT
WON BY
MERICK LANGE
AWARDED BY
MASTERCRAFTSMEN JEWELERS
DES MOINES, IOWA

TE FAIR

TARY.

PRESIDENT

Iowa.

August

DEAR

with our An
venth Exhibiti
held at Des Mo
ith, inclusive
We re
will
ce you
he Fi

AUG. 23 - SEPT. 1, 1916

STATE STOCK FOOD AND EXHIBITION
DES MOINES

CATTLE DEPARTM
RED POLLED

FOURTH PRIZE

1ST PRIZE
PRODUCE OF DUROC JERSEY SOW
IOWA STATE FAIR, 1914

D NAUMAN & SON

THE ECONOMY HOG & CATTLE POWDER CO

or a subscription to an agricultural periodical; first-place winners received diplomas. A monetary premium was only given when "the case rendered it indispensable" to do otherwise. (Sorry, but we don't know what the society meant by that!)

The awarding of premiums and diplomas with no money attached didn't last long, however. The ISAS had incorrectly assumed that Iowans' sense of pride would sufficiently motivate them to compete. Quite frankly, it appears that Iowans in the 19th century were more interested in cold, hard cash than a "testimonial of advertised value." As Society President George Wright observed in 1864, "While men ought to be, and in many instances I know are, actuated by other than merely sordid motives, yet without the money inducement we are satisfied that the gates of our fair grounds would rust upon their hinges and our halls decay from non-use."

How much money you took home depended more upon the year in which you won than upon the quality of your creation. That's because the premium money came from the society's treasury; some years the coffers were fat, and other years they were lean. So lean, in fact, that there wasn't always enough money to go around!

WILLOWHURST

IOWA NEVER FAILS

HILDEBRAND

THE PROBLEM WITH JUDGES

The problem with moneyless premiums was only an annoyance compared with the issue of who should judge the competition. In the beginning, the judges were judged to be the problem. Sometimes, the judges didn't show up on time; other times, they didn't show up at all. And often, the judges weren't knowledgeable about the categories they were judging. Not surprisingly, this caused exhibitors to wrangle, whine, rail and generally make unkind remarks about the capacity of certain persons to judge anything at all. In an 1863 message, the ISAS President George Wright suggested judges turn a deaf ear to such exhibitors, unless responding to one of their questions. "Close your eyes, ears and consciences to all else, save the actual, positive, legitimate, practical merits of the articles submitted for your examination," he said. "Discard fully and entirely all possible feeling or prejudice. Never think for a moment of how your decisions will affect this man or that. Maintain at all times your own self-respect, and secure the approval of your own honest judgments."

Nice advice, but it didn't solve any problems. By the 1880s, exhibitors were complaining so much about the need for quality judges that the ISAS began selecting knowledgeable judges (even going out of state to find them), charging entry fees to eliminate exhibitors who weren't serious, restricting the number of items displayed to ensure more quality, and giving consideration to how the entry looked—its "presentation."

WORTHY WINNERS

Here's a sampling of what judges in the early 1860s deemed superior:

• A diploma and $100 went to the best and fastest trotting stallion, but only $10 was awarded for the best breaking plow pulled by oxen.

• The designer of the best plans for a district schoolhouse (not to cost more than $600) received a diploma and $5.

• Men could match their oxcarts for a $5 prize or their two-horse rollers and clod crushers for $4.

• Farmers so inclined competed for money by writing an essay on some phase of agriculture. However, no manuscript could be longer than eight pages of foolscap [a 13X16-inch sheet of writing paper].

• Miss Agnes W. Cowgill of Johnson County was awarded the first premium for the best yeast bread and pound of butter. According to the ISAS report, "We hope young bachelors will make a note of this.... We regret that we have not the names of the other young ladies, who wrung such praises from the committee, in order that we might publish them."

• The 1861 State Fair offered a popular farm magazine to anyone receiving a premium of $5 or more.

• Two bottles of Catawba, grape, currant, blackberry, elderberry or rhubarb wine brought $1 for the winner. But it took six bottles of good cider to win that much, and neither cider nor wine makers got a diploma.

• J.S. Charles of Marion received a diploma for superior dental work. (We can only assume he was a dentist.)

Today, all of that is standard practice. Every year, superintendents in each department hire their own judges. How many they hire will vary, depending upon the number of entries received, but about 375 persons hand out ribbons annually for competition in 7,500 different classes. Judges of horses, livestock and certain categories in the fabric, photography, fine arts and creative arts departments are paid professionals. Judges in the food, heritage, 4-H and FFA herdsmanship and showmanship, and the Cowgirl Queen categories also are paid but don't necessarily work full-time in the field. Finally, there are knowledgeable people who volunteer their time to judge. Then there are local celebrities who are neither paid nor knowledgeable in the areas they're judging. But they sure have fun deciding which contestants do the best job of throwing cow chips (real, but sanitized, to which we still say, "Eeeeh-yuwww!").

We don't know where the idea of throwing a cow chip originated (nor why anyone would *want* to throw one), but we do know some things about other categories of State Fair competition:

• You can compete by stitching a quilt, calling a hog, playing stupendous checkers, designing a floral arrangement with cut or dried flowers, knitting an afghan, snapping a picture, growing pretty apples, or entering a potato you grew that looks for all the world like a U.S. President. (Suggestions for new categories come from entrants and superintendents.)

• You used to be able to compete by latch-hooking a rug, answering tough questions, collecting fossils, macraméing anything, sewing the prettiest scrap bag or building a display out of flour sacks. But all those contests have been eliminated for lack of participation. (When is the last time you even saw a flour sack?) (continued on page 72)

Madelyn Levitt

• If you want to visit the most popular competitions—photography and food—you may have to wait in line just to squeeze into the exhibit area.

• Some contestants bring a single entry; others haul in a truckload.

• Some competitions require you to register ahead of time; with others, all you have to do is show up.

• Sometimes, you win a ribbon and money; other times, you win nothing. Winning the ribbon and money is preferable, but it's all fun.

Where do all these contestants come from? Some find the State Fair; others are found by the State Fair. For example, the Fair sends representatives to wood shows, seminars and clubs throughout Iowa, urging carvers to compete. And compete they do, using everything from dentists' drills and pneumatic professional tools to knives and gouges (that's like a carpenter's chisel).

Nine-year-old Jennifer Ober of Spring Hill once carved a turtle with the help of her grandfather, Jerry Wilson of Des Moines. (Word is that she accepted Grandpa's advice as long as he didn't actually touch the turtle.) Jaleen Herman of Pleasant Hill, who had only been carving for nine months, took home a blue ribbon for her little elf standing on a maple leaf. Then there was the Chariton man, whose entry wasn't dry when it was time to drive to the Fair. So his wife held the piece up to the open window all the way to Des Moines.

And a favorite story is told about Bill Musgrove of Reasnor. While spending the '98–'99 winter season in McAllen, Texas, Mr. Musgrove carved a caricature of a little old lady wearing a bonnet and shawl. He intended to enter it the following summer in State Fair competition, (continued on page 76)

FINE FINE ART

Once upon a time, Iowa's favorite artist, Grant Wood, came to the Fair. Well, actually, Mr. Wood came to the Fair several times and, not surprisingly, he took all sorts of grand prize and blue ribbon honors back to Cedar Rapids with him.

He first entered "John D. Turner, Pioneer" in the 1929 Art Salon competition. By then, Mr. Wood already had lived and studied in Europe and was moving away from the traditional European style of painting toward what would come to be called regionalism. Those persons in charge of the Art Salon favored the traditional approach and had been trying for several years to keep any "modern art" influences out of the State Fair (and out of the state, actually). In fact, J. Laurie Wallace of Omaha, who judged the 1925 Fair entries, said, "I have no sympathy for most of this modernist stuff," adding that artistic "vogues" such as Picasso, Matisse and Gauguin would soon be gone and forgotten.

So, what was a fellow like Grant Wood—who paints perfectly round hills even if they aren't really round— doing in the Art Salon? Truth is, the Fair's Art Salon was the best-attended art exhibit in the whole state. Plus, Grant Wood painted Iowa, and did it so well, we might add, that after four years of grand sweeps, he voluntarily withdrew from competition, but continued to display his work. Even then, students in his Stone City artist colony continued to walk off with Fair honors, as did colleague and fellow regionalist Marvin Cone.

In 1936, Dan Rhodes of Fort Dodge—who was left of left in the regionalist movement—won the grand prize for "Painters." Two years later, Rhodes and another regionalist named Howard Johnson painted a mural on wood in the Agriculture Building as a WPA (Works Progress Administration) project. In 1946, only eight years later, the mural was torn down, cut up and used to repair buildings.

but he died before the Fair began. So his wife requested the carving be entered posthumously. The judge—appropriately enough a caricature carver of national acclaim—awarded Mr. Musgrove's little old lady not only a blue ribbon but also the Caricature Carver of America Award.

Can't carve anything except the end of your thumb? That's okay. You probably have other talents. Like whistling. Bill Phillips, a Chicago lawyer, whistled at the 1987 Fair. Thing was, Mr. Phillips wasn't planning on whistling in public that day. He and his wife had been touring the Amana Colonies when he spotted a newspaper schedule of State Fair events. "And there it was, a whistling contest," he says. "I thought to myself, why not enter? I'm from the Windy City."

So the couple drove 100 miles to the State Fair, where Mr. Phillips wowed about 250 folks gathered to hear seven whistlers—six adults and one very brave 7-year-old who got all the way through "Pop Goes the Weasel." Mr. Phillips faced tough competition from blue-ribbon whistler Lo McGilva, 77, who started performing at the age of 5 and had whistled with a band that played summer concerts on the grounds of the Iowa State Capitol. Mr. Phillips performed a rousing Sousa march that demanded fluttering high notes, booming low notes and deep breaths in between. (Even Mrs. McGilva cheered him on.) For his efforts, Mr. Phillips won a red ribbon.

Can't carve anything except the end of your thumb? That's okay. You probably have other talents. Like whistling.

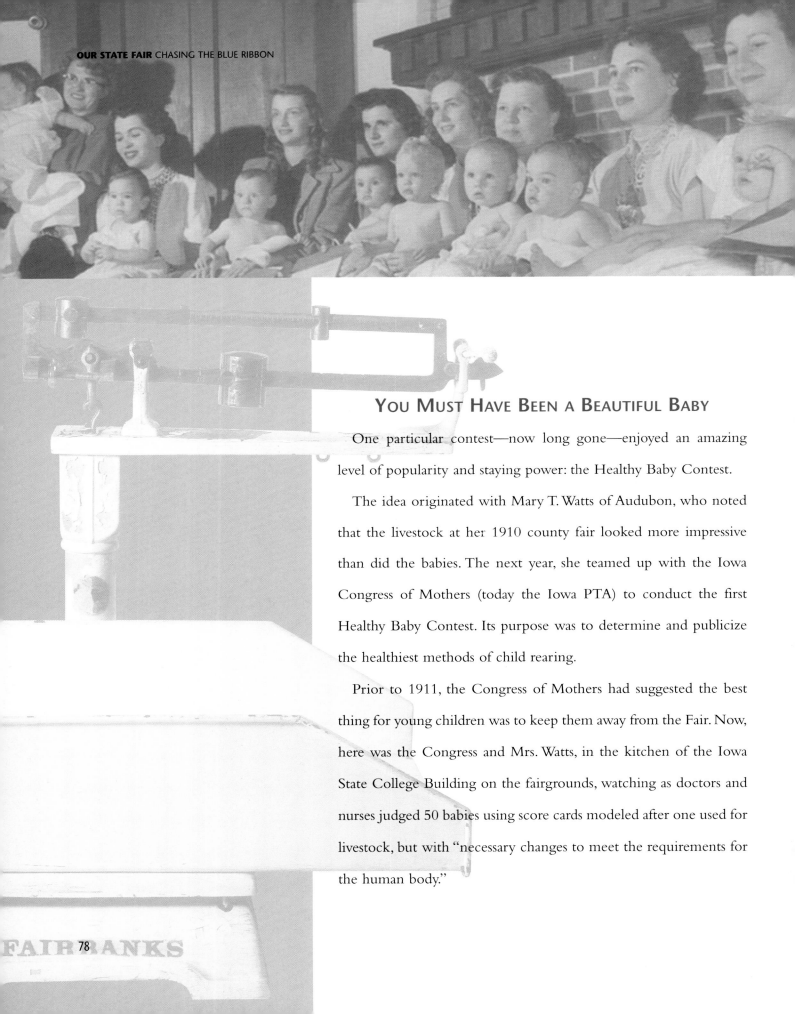

YOU MUST HAVE BEEN A BEAUTIFUL BABY

One particular contest—now long gone—enjoyed an amazing level of popularity and staying power: the Healthy Baby Contest.

The idea originated with Mary T. Watts of Audubon, who noted that the livestock at her 1910 county fair looked more impressive than did the babies. The next year, she teamed up with the Iowa Congress of Mothers (today the Iowa PTA) to conduct the first Healthy Baby Contest. Its purpose was to determine and publicize the healthiest methods of child rearing.

Prior to 1911, the Congress of Mothers had suggested the best thing for young children was to keep them away from the Fair. Now, here was the Congress and Mrs. Watts, in the kitchen of the Iowa State College Building on the fairgrounds, watching as doctors and nurses judged 50 babies using score cards modeled after one used for livestock, but with "necessary changes to meet the requirements for the human body."

FAIRBANKS

The State Fair contest was an instant hit. The next year—1912—lectures and exhibitors were added. For days, "skilled physicians especially qualified for making such examinations" weighed, measured, punched, poked and tested 230 youngsters under the age of 3 in front of a glass wall. On the other side, everybody from anxious parents to curious fairgoers jockeyed for a view. Prizes amounting to $280 were awarded to the most perfect babies in the various classes.

By 1915, judges were able to examine 72 babies each day, and even then, plenty of parents were disappointed to learn that they arrived too late to enter their offspring in competition. The Fair Board reported, "We observe that, although the fathers of the contesting babies speak of the matter with rather good-natured tolerance or adopt a bored expression, they may be found anxiously hovering about just outside of the circle of spectators watching every movement made by the judges."

By the early 1920s, entries were limited to 700, and the contest was spawning all sorts of situations:

• Dr. Charles Seashore, a professor of psychology at the State University of Iowa, announced his intention to develop a graduate-level course in baby judging.

• A mental test was added to make sure the winners were of sound mind as well as sound body.

IOWA STATE FAIR
1937
GRAND CHAMPION
BABY HEALTH BOY
WON BY
DONALD EUGENE ABRAN

"Popularizing health until it is really quite the thing to be strong and well will do much toward lessening the reproduction of defectives. As our young people grow up they see the beauty of this much-talked-of health perfection and select mates who have the qualities they have been led to admire. The contest will foster this idea of health and beauty being synonymous and so should be encouraged."

Mary Watts, 1914

STANDARD SCORE CARD FOR BABIES
ISSUED BY
THE AMERICAN MEDICAL ASSOCIATION
CHICAGO, ILLINOIS

Total score 97½
Entry No. 621

Name .. Bolen Dora .... Address .. Malcom, Ia ....

Male ....
Female .. ✓ .... } Class {
City .... Age in months .. 24, 23 ......
Town .... Age division .. 24, 32 ......
Rural

Weight at birth .. 9 .. Lbs. .. 5 .. Oz.
Father's name .. Warren M. Bellon ......

Condition at birth: Strong .. ✓ .. Feeble ....
Address .. Malcom .. Age .. 25 ..
Nationality .. Amer ..

No. of child of mother: 1, 2, 3, 4, 5, 6, 7, 8, 9, 10th child ....
Occupation .. Farmer ..

Breast fed .. ✓ .. How many months .. 7 mo ..
Mother's maiden name .. Connie Garden ..
Nationality .. Amer .. Age .. 22 ..

Bottle and breast fed .... How many months ....
Has birth been registered .. ✓ ..

Bottle fed .. ✓ .. How many months .. 5 ..
Where .. Brooklyn ..

What foods .. Mod milk ..
If not, why ....

Kinds of food at present .. Family Diet ..
Baby sleeps alone .. ✓ ..

No. of feedings in 24 hours .... 3 ..
If not, with whom ....

Ounces of food at each feeding .. 8 oz milk ....
Sleeps in open air .... Day .... Night ....

Examination held at .. Iowa State Fair .. By .. Baby Health Center .. Date .. 9/3/25 ..
Windows open, how many .. 3 ..

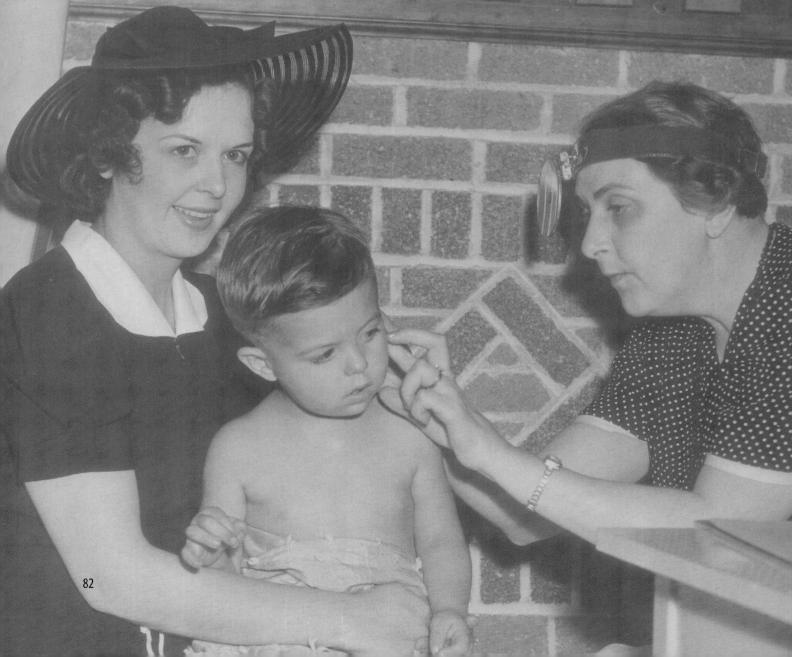

82

• A baby specialist was on duty to consult with mothers, and the State University of Iowa conducted a free clinic for "crippled, deformed or underdeveloped" children.

• The "Iowa idea" spread across this country.

• It was assumed that the winners would be from rural areas, but those little city kids were crawling and toddling off with first-place honors. The *Iowa Homestead* decided that was because the judges were mostly "city-bred folks."

The contest kept up a healthy pace until 1949, when it was cancelled as a precaution against the spread of infantile paralysis (polio). In fact, until August 13 of that summer, there was discussion about whether to close down the entire Fair (which did not happen). When the contest was reinstated the following year, each contestant was placed in three categories: 1) boy or girl; 2) age 12 to 24 months or 24 to 33 months; and 3) city/town (2,500 to 15,000) or farm resident. The healthiest boy and girl each hauled home a grand champion trophy, and the twins who scored highest in their own classes each received silver porridge dishes.

The contest was cancelled again in 1952, this time because of the shortage of volunteer physicians. It was never reinstated.

TIP-TOP TEENAGERS

In 1919, Dr. Caroline Hedger of Dubuque noted that the Fair awarded a "blue ribbon for the steer but none for the lad," and what do you know! Contests to find the state's healthiest teenage boy and girl were launched. This time, nobody pitted the city mouse against the country mouse since only 4-H-ers could enter.

The contestants were viewed under a microscope, so to speak. Consider the report card of 15-year-old Alberta Hoppe, the 1926 girls champion who lived on a farm south of Cedar Rapids:

"Doctors in the final examination of Alberta scored off .03 for irregular teeth and for malocclusion; .1 for abnormal eyelids; .2 for enlarged glands; .2 for slight irregularities of form; .2 for antero-posterior curvature of the spine; .2 for irregularity of her feet and legs and .2 for her gait."

The winners portrayed what were called "rural virtues." For example, it was noted that Miss Hoppe "has never worn a corset or a high heeled shoe. She uses no powder or rouge, cares nothing for boys and dates, does not dance and rarely goes to movies." The boy winners always wanted to stay on the farm.

The Youth Contest was never as popular as the Healthy Baby Contest and was phased out by the late 1930s.

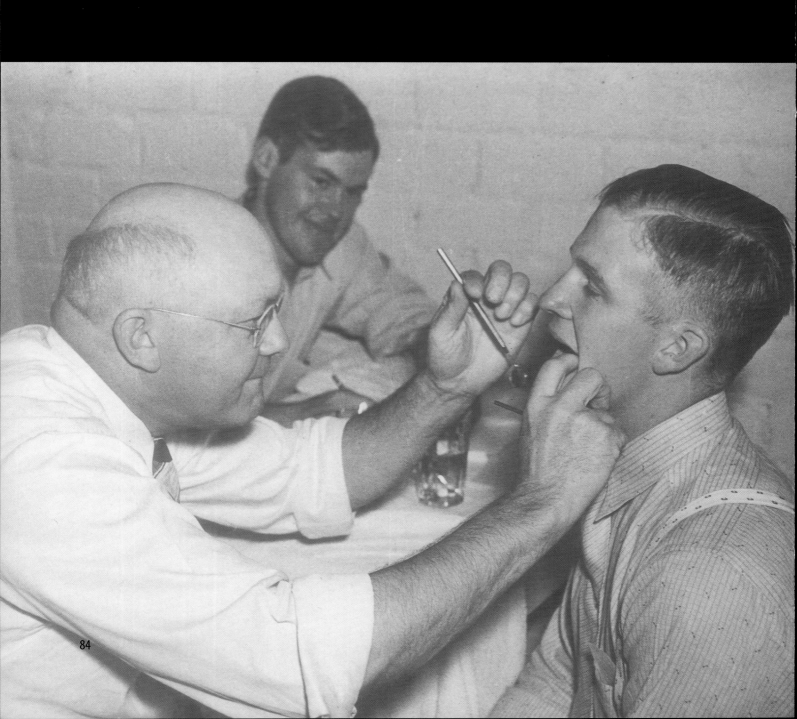

IOWA STATE FAIR
4-H CLUB
MEMBER
DES MOINES

A ROYAL EXPERIENCE

It's great to be the queen! Not easy, perhaps, but great. So great, in fact, that over the decades, thousands and thousands of young ladies have sought the coveted title, Queen of the Iowa State Fair. Back in 1922—when the contest was open to every girl in Iowa no matter where she lived—6,200 entered. Considered for their beauty and tested for character, refinement and womanliness, the luckiest young women kept advancing until, finally, one from each Congressional district went to the State Fair. The judging and coronation took several days, with the winner receiving $1,000 in gold; the others received prizes in proportion to their standing in the contest.

By 1950, pageant sponsors *The Des Moines Register* and the Iowa State Fair were looking only for the "most representative farm girl." (The farm had to be at least 80 acres.) The winner and her mother received a trip to California on a special train with several hundred former-Iowans-turned-Californians.

Today's State Fair Queen Pageant—which provides equal opportunity for city and country girls—dates back to 1963 when Fair Secretary Ken Fulk said to Helen Deets, "I'd like to add a pageant to the Fair. Would you run it for a year or two?" Mrs. Deets, whose husband was maintenance superintendent at the time, said yes; 16 years later, she relinquished those duties to open the Iowa State Fair Museum.

Some things have changed since the '60s. Back then, contestants stayed downtown at the Kirkwood Hotel, until so many got sidetracked by department stores that the (continued on page 90)

In 1939, actress (and redhead) Susan Hayward came to the State Fair to help judge the Queen of the Redheads contest, which lasted four days. Twenty-five women participated in the finals in front of the Grandstand. Six of them were awarded official movie screen tests; Queen Margaret Leeper of Waterloo received a free trip to Hollywood where she was Miss Hayward's guest.

The judging and coronation took several days, with the winner receiving $1,000 in gold; the others received prizes in proportion to their standing in the contest.

contestants were moved to Johnny and Kay's Hyatt House, out by the airport. Today, the queen and her chaperone stay in an apartment in the Administration Building. Another change from the '60s—back then, most contestants had never been to the State Fair, let alone stayed in a motel. Today, few fit that profile.

One thing hasn't changed since the '60s. The young women were declared to be absolutely wonderful then. (Mrs. Deets sent only two home early in her 16-year tenure.) And they are still wonderful today, according to Brenda Annett, a 1990s keeper of the candidates. Each year, she shepherded 90-plus young women though competition, then helped the queen with her official duties for the duration of the Fair. That included making appearances, attending events, serving as a judge, doing interviews with the media and working with the vendors.

Ms. Annett knew what she was doing because in 1985 Brenda Annett of West Des Moines was Brenda Johnson of Alleman, who was having a lot of fun as a Fair Queen candidate but never thought of winning. At the coronation ceremony, she was sitting in the front row on the stage when the State Fair Board president announced that the winner was Brenda Joelson. "I was just thinking that I hadn't yet met Brenda Joelson," says Ms. Annett, "when the girl next to me leaned over, started shaking me and said, 'He mispronounced that name. You're the winner!'"

IN SEARCH OF TALENT

Back in 1946, it was One Big Deal.

A New York RCA camera crew set up a television broadcast studio and control room in the International Harvester tent at the Iowa State Fair. Inside the tent were several "home television receivers"—with screens measuring about 12 inches. Each day of the Fair, Des Moines radio station KRNT presented variety shows live from the stage. Fairgoers jammed inside the tent to view the show being televised on the stage and pictured on the TV sets at the same time!

The emcee for the variety shows, by the way, was Bill Riley.

It was the Iowa Falls native's first time hosting a show at the State Fair, although he already was producing a talent show for KRNT Radio. For the next three decades, he continued to produce talent shows for KRNT Radio and then, KRNT-TV. He also reported the news and sports. At one point, he was doing 21 radio and television shows a week.

But it was always Iowa's talented young people who most fascinated him. Finally, in 1957, he approached Fair Secretary Lloyd Cunningham about showcasing the kids during the State Fair. It took two years of convincing, but in 1959, Bill Riley's first State Fair Talent Search was a go. By August of that year, Mr. Riley had crisscrossed the state, holding countless talent shows and raising thousands of dollars for school groups at the same time. Now, the créme de la créme were ready for prime time—

appearing on an old wooden stage by a big tree in the extreme southwest corner of the fairgrounds.

"Our daily shows started at 2 o'clock," Mr. Riley recalls. "They were so popular that people weren't attending the afternoon shows in the Grandstand, so the Fair Board asked us to move our start time to 1 o'clock. Then, people went on to the Grandstand, but they got there late. So finally, we started our shows at noon."

Thirty-nine years later, Mr. Riley retired.

It was 1996 and, by then, he'd seen it all. Unicyclers and jugglers, accordion players and baton twirlers, singers and dancers, pianists and violinists—and, of course, the young man from Johnston who stood at one end of the stage with a black

snake whip and his assistant, who stood at the other end with a piece of paper rolled up between her lips. His "act" was to snap the whip and pop the paper out of his assistant's mouth. (The assistant was his mother.)

By then, the shows were held on the Bill Riley Stage (formerly the Plaza Stage) directly south of the Administration Building. This included seven days of preliminaries for both the Sprouts (ages 2–12) and the Seniors (ages 13–21), followed by the semifinals and, ultimately, the selection of six Sprouts champions and one Seniors champion. All told, Riley's efforts put about 150 acts gathered from county fairs and local talent events on the State Fair stage every year.

By the time he retired, he'd raised money for almost every cause you could think of—including construction of the Science Center of Iowa in Des Moines and the Bill Riley Trail and the Blank Park Zoo.

By then, he was affectionately known as Mr. State Fair.

It took two people to replace him on the State Fair stage that was named after him—son Bill of Des Moines and Terry Rich of Urbandale.

WHAT A LINEUP!

"*The day of the American people is past to look upon pumpkins and small onions. We are living in a fast age, and attractions and humbugs are the order of the day. The bigger the humbug, the more we take to it. We hope to give such an exhibition that will please and tickle people.*"

J.M. Shaffer, Fair Secretary, 1880

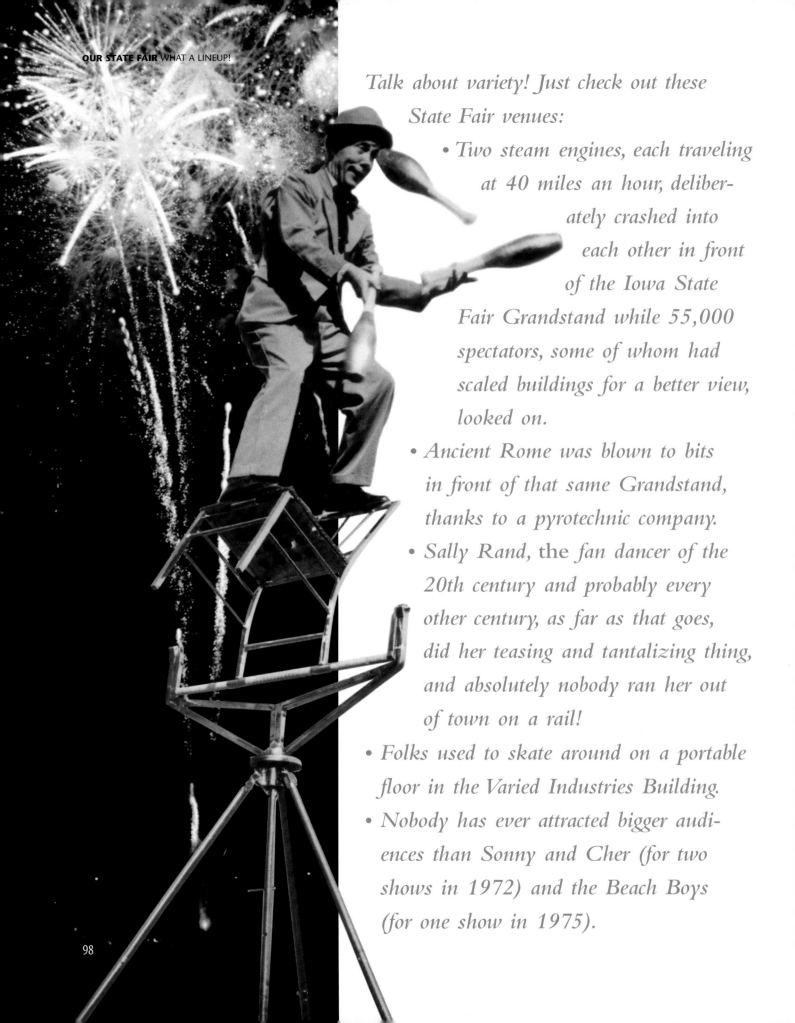

Talk about variety! Just check out these State Fair venues:

- *Two steam engines, each traveling at 40 miles an hour, deliberately crashed into each other in front of the Iowa State Fair Grandstand while 55,000 spectators, some of whom had scaled buildings for a better view, looked on.*

- *Ancient Rome was blown to bits in front of that same Grandstand, thanks to a pyrotechnic company.*

- *Sally Rand, the fan dancer of the 20th century and probably every other century, as far as that goes, did her teasing and tantalizing thing, and absolutely nobody ran her out of town on a rail!*

- *Folks used to skate around on a portable floor in the Varied Industries Building.*

- *Nobody has ever attracted bigger audiences than Sonny and Cher (for two shows in 1972) and the Beach Boys (for one show in 1975).*

You can bet that at that first Iowa State Fair in 1854, such notions of entertainment weren't even a twinkle in somebody's eye! People went to see livestock (including a mule "16 hands high"), grains and new farm tools—not to mention fruits, needlework and weaving. They shared experiences and competed for ribbons awarded for "meritorious exertion." But did they come to be entertained?

Nope.

TO MY BELOVED SUBJECTS!

The Great King Sends Greeting:

DAY HAS DAWNED! Night with her dark overshadowing Wings flees away. The Great King calls to his waiting and faithful subjects! Up! Shake sleep from your drowsy eyelids! Awake! Awake! From the far off and Mysterious Isle, never gazed upon by the eye of Man he comes to reign and to set one of the Stars of the Empire in her course again! Too long has her Chariot Wheels driven heavily!

The Great King of Seni Om Sed has so Decreed! He has Spoken! He has Uttered his Voice and it shall be Done!

Hear ye all my Children; ye of the Soil Stained Palms; ye who with faces begrimed, toil in Subterranean Regions; ye who toil at the Bench; ye who toil at the Forge; ye workers in Metals; ye Hewers of Wood and Drawers of Water; ye who buy and sell and get gain; ye Scribes; ye Physicians; ye tillers of the Soil; ye Money Changers; ye Men in High Places; ye Red Men of the Primeval Forests; ye Sons from Africa's Burning Sands; ye Sons from the Hyperborean Regions; and all who hear his Voice:

The Great King will reveal himself and make known his further desires, seated on his Regal Throne drawn by beautifully caparisoned steeds, amid Bursting Bombs and Lightning borrowed from the skies, causing Fair Luna to hide her face and the stars to veil themselves in his presence.

Therefore, all to whom this writing shall be made known, throughout the whole Land are commanded and required to appear before him at Des Moines, Iowa, September 2, 3, 4 and 5, 1889, to pay their Homage and receive his Wise and Supreme Commands.

By order of the Great King:

SENI OM SED.

Remember the Date
DES MOINES, SEPT. 2·3·4·5
4 ◆ FOUR GALA NIGHTS ◆ 4

The Iowa State Agricultural Society (ISAS), the Fair's sponsor until 1902, believed that such annual expositions would enable farmers, manufacturers and homemakers to learn from one another and teach one another. Additionally, competition would spur Iowans to improve the quality of their products—which ultimately would

1897 **IOWA STATE** 1897

Agricultural ∘ Society
AND INDUSTRIAL EXPOSITION.
FORTY-FOURTH ANNUAL

STATE FAIR

STATE FAIR GROUNDS
DES MOINES, SEPT'R 9 to 18

$30,000 PREMIUMS

Exhibits in all departments will be greater than at any previous exhibition. Every hall will have some new attractive feature.

ATTRACTIONS.

Model Indian Village (reproduction of the one shown at World's Fair); the Winnebagoes and Sacs and Foxes will play for the championship in the Indian's game of La Crosse; Dr. Carver, champion shot of the world, in his marvelous feats; high-diving horses plunge from tower thirty feet high into lake twelve feet deep; Kemp Sisters' Wild West Show, thrilling exhibition of wild frontier life, genuine western Cowboy, fancy rifle shooting; Chariot Races, Hurdle Races, Roman Races; Fancy Drills and Dress Parades by Patriarchs Militant, I. O. O. F.; one thousand School Children Drill and March; Old Soldiers' Camp Fires.

THE RACES
$7,500 IN PURSES.

Three Heat Races have been adopted in the Speed Department, every heat a race. Many of the swift-goers will be on the track.

SPEED PROGRAM.

MONDAY. SEPT. 13.	PURSE	WEDNESDAY, SEPT. 15.	PURSE	FRIDAY, SEPT. 17.	
2:50 Trotting	$300	2:20 Trotting	$800	2:35 Trotting	$400
2:35 Pacing (3 yr. old)	300	2:10 Pacing	500	2:17 Pacing	800
2:50 Trotting (2 yr. old)	250	Running (half mile heats)	200	Running (mile heats)	500
TUESDAY, SEPT. 14.		**THURSDAY, SEPT. 16.**		**SATURDAY, SEPT. 18.**	
2:24 Pacing	$400	2:50 Pacing (2 yr. old)	$250	2:29 Pacing	$400
2:25 Trotting	400	2:40 Pacing	400	Trotting (free for all)	500
2:38 Trotting (3 yr. old)	300	2:15 Trotting	500	Running (3-4 mile dash)	100
		Running (half mile dash)	100		

THE RACES WILL BE FIRST CLASS
IN EVERY PARTICULAR.

SENI OM SED
CARNIVAL.

DES MOINES will throw down the bars and extend a royal welcome to all who come. The City to be bathed in a brilliant blaze of

SENI-OM-SED
(READ IT BACKWARDS)

Q: Was Seni-Om-Sed good for the Iowa State Fair?

A: We don't know. But we can report that the early 1890s weren't so good for the Fair—with or without Seni-Om-Sed.

Seni-Om-Sed (Des Moines spelled backwards) was a carnival the Des Moines business community first sponsored in 1889. (It reappeared as a Friday night, downtown celebration toward the end of the 20th century.) In 1889, it ran the same week as the Iowa State Fair, so visitors could enjoy the fairgrounds as well as Des Moines. It also highlighted a concern addressed in an *Iowa State Register* editorial stating that it "will not do to limit [the Fair] to a horse and cattle show, to an exclusively agricultural show, to a speed exhibition or to any one idea or interest. Let it be the great bazaar, the great exposition of all Iowa's material interests." In other words, the Fair needed to meld city and country—and holding Seni-Om-Sed in the same city during the same week as the Fair was a beginning.

Seni-Om-Sed featured a parade, the King of Harvest, a street fair, bands, fireworks, addresses, a bicycle brigade and a mock battle with veterans of the Grand Army Posts. At night, thousands of electric lights in colored glass globes arranged in many artistic forms lit up downtown. It was such a production that one writer wondered after the first Seni-Om-Sed if the event might not come to rival New Orleans' Mardi Gras or St. Louis' Veiled Prophet celebrations.

The business community staged a second Seni-Om-Sed in 1890, plus they erected the Des Moines Producers Hall on the fairgrounds. Des Moines manufacturers displayed their wares, from carriages to wood pumps to typewriters to blankets. In those days, you could buy local from the cradle to the grave.

(continued on page 103)

101

increase Iowa's prestige in the national marketplace. There was no need for a grandstand, a midway or a free stage; no call for accordion players, puppeteers or Clydesdales parading on the Grand Concourse; no reason for pig races, tractor pulls or Chuck Berry.

But you know what? From the beginning, there *was* entertainment at the Iowa State Fair—whether the ISAS liked it or not. Dogs and bears fought; alligators crawled; the organgrinder played while his monkey collected coins; freak shows, games of chance and snake oil salesmen leered and lured. In an effort to separate their Fair from such riffraff, the ISAS required entertainers to remain outside the wooden fence surrounding the fairgrounds—which merely proved that you can take the entertainment out of the fairgrounds but you can't take it away from the fairgoer. On their way inside, folks would stop and shop. With all the money-changing going on outside the fence, the ISAS received no cut from the profits. Consequently, the Society began to invite some of the "quality" entertainers to set up inside the

(continued from page 101)

Whether the Iowa State Agricultural Society viewed Des Moines as being supportive of its Fair or in competition with it, we can't say. Whether Des Moines intended to augment the Fair or promote itself, we can't say. We do know that in 1893, the Fair had to deal with the Columbian Exposition in Chicago, a drought and a depression. Plus, Des Moines replaced Seni-Om-Sed with a 10-day festival, culminating each evening with the destruction of Pompeii via fireworks. Because of that, the Fair experienced such profound losses that the ISAS president said, "In relation to the destruction of Pompeii, [I] hope that when it is again destroyed it will not occur in Des Moines during the time of our Fair, for I am confident that it took many thousands of dollars which, had it not been here, would have come to us during the day."

The next year, during the financially beleaguered State Fair run, the Barnum and Bailey Circus came to Des Moines!

But there was some good news. It's believed those Seni-Om-Sed parades were the precursor to today's State Fair Parade, the kick-off to the Fair. The largest parade in Iowa, it attracts about 100,000 spectators who clap their hands and tap their toes as floats, marching bands, novelty and animal units pass by.

MAGNIFICENT NIGHT PAGEANT,
The Siege of Vicksburg

Realistic River Scenes, with Trained Troops, Gunboats, Hot Shot and Shell, Booming Cannon, True Representation of the Terrible Time.

GLITTERING
Spectacular ★ Parade

Abounding in magnificent masterpieces of historic character. Finest floats on wheels. Decorated cars.

GROTESQUE
Burlesque Procession

Miles of mirth-making, side splitting caricatures. Crowning of the Clown. Fun run riot.

In 1895, a mock battle was fought between Ames cadets and two companies of the Iowa National Guard. However, the Woman's Christian Temperance Union strongly objected to the battle, saying it was "not in harmony with the true spirit of Christian civilization."

fence—but at a respectable distance from the agricultural exhibits, thus giving the Society both revenue and control.

In 1880, the second year the Fair was in Des Moines, the Society contracted for its first major entertainment act, paying $400 for a Roman chariot race. J.M. Shaffer, Fair secretary, explained the shift toward paid entertainment: "The day of the American people is past to look upon pumpkins and small onions. We are living in a fast age, and attractions and humbugs are the order of the day. The bigger the humbug, the more we take to it. We hope to give such an exhibition that will please and tickle people."

Mr. Shaffer was right on target. The chariot race proved popular enough to be restaged for several more years. And wow! What followed in its wake—musicals, rodeos, racing, operas, all sorts of flying demonstrations and Willie Nelson.

But wait! We're getting ahead of ourselves. The outdoor entertainment movement was a hit-and-miss proposition up to the latter part of the 19th century. Its transformation into a bona fide industry began with the 1893 Columbian Exposition in Chicago. After that World's Fair was over, a lot of entertainers were roaming around the country looking for more work—and that spawned booking agents, large carnival companies, fair circuits and associations of fair managers.

And so it was that entertainment came to our State Fair.

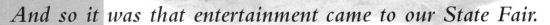

104

ON WITH THE SHOW...

There were always horse races at the Fair, but they weren't always entertaining—or at least they weren't supposed to be. In the beginning, such races were referred to as "trials of speed"—one of many competitive events meant to highlight good stock. Horse racing per se was against the law.

Still, not everyone bought into that fine line between legal trials of speed and illegal horse racing. Finally, in 1881, the Iowa Supreme Court ruled that an agricultural society's job was to "offer premiums [prize money] for the improvement of stock." In this case, the premiums happened to be based on speed. And, the ruling concluded, the responsibility of awarding premiums took precedence over the Iowa Code's ban on racing.

So, horses raced (or participated in trials of speed, if you will). But betting was not allowed for another century. Movement in that direction began in 1981, when fairgoers could "Pick the Winner" for a cash prize during two big afternoons of free harness racing. Fans made their choices on special forms distributed in the Grandstand, and the Iowa Horsemen's Association awarded $10 to one winner per race.

Well, you know how one thing leads to another! In 1983, the Legislature legalized pari-mutuel betting and established the Iowa Racing Commission (now the Iowa Racing and Gaming Commission). Discussion ensued about adding a clubhouse at the Grandstand and enlarging the racetrack to five-eighths of a mile to accommodate a 60-day racing season. But when a license was issued in 1984 for construction of a place to be called Prairie Meadows, plans for Grandstand changes dissipated. (Continued on page 110)

One of the Sensations in the
"GREAT CARVER SHOW"

THOSE LADIES ON HORSEBACK

Back in 1854, 10 ladies brought their riding horses to the first State Fair. Interesting, since not everyone thought an Iowa lady belonged on the back of a horse—at least not in public. And they said so often and loudly. Nevertheless, when it came time for the ladies to perform in riding competition, thousands gathered 'round to watch. First prize was a lady's gold hunting watch, offered by Judge Thomas Clagett, a member of the Iowa State Agricultural Society and a founding father of the Fair.

Each lady was to ride once around the circle, accompanied by a gentleman trained in horsemanship. That completed, her cavalier would walk to the center of the circle to wait while she rode four times around at any speed she might choose.

This she performed by herself! Finally, the cavalier rejoined his lady, leading both her and her horse out of the ring.

According to newspaper reports that first year, 13-year-old Eliza Jane Hodges of Iowa City caused her horse to gallop, trot, canter and end in a lively charge. As you may expect, Miss Hodges received much cheering. It was also written that Miss Belle Turner from Keokuk was graceful, skillful and with elegant form, not to mention her fine face and soft blue eyes. No mention was made of her galloping, trotting or cantering.

At the end of the competition, fairgoers demanded more, so a second competition was added to the next day's agenda. Much to the crowd's delight, Miss Hodges of Iowa City turned

out to be even more thrilling, fearless and magnificent than the day before—which is probably why everyone was so surprised when first place went to the graceful Miss Turner of Keokuk. The judges' decision caused a great deal of clamoring that ended with fairgoers collecting $165 for the also-ran Miss Hodges.

So, in the end, Miss Turner took home the ladies' gold hunting watch, and Miss Hodges took home enough money to attend three terms at the Female Seminary at Fairfield and one term at the new college at Mount Pleasant, most likely Mt. Pleasant Collegiate Institute which is now Iowa Wesleyan College.

Even so, beginning in 1985, the Commission okayed pari-mutuel wagering on harness racing at the State Fair and several county fairs; betting windows were installed in the Grandstand, and the horses were off!

Still, pari-mutuel betting at the Fair didn't generate enough participation to be considered successful, probably because folks were waiting for Prairie Meadows Racetrack to open in Altoona.

Consequently, four years after the betting windows opened at the fairgrounds, they closed; the next year, Prairie Meadows was off and running.

There is still harness racing at our State Fair, as well as at some county fairs, but betting is not allowed.

Speaking of horses and such, the first rodeo—Cheyenne Frontier Days—performed on the racetrack in 1912 under 250-candlepower electric lights (90 of them) and three floodlights. Wild West rodeos were a major attraction in the '30s, '40s and '50s. Sometimes, it required three or four consecutive nights, including the big-draw nights of Saturday and Sunday, to get all those broncos ridden, calves roped and steers wrestled.

Gene Autry and Champion (oh, surely you know who Champion was!) helped celebrate the State Fair Centennial in 1954.

DAN PATCH

Perhaps the most famous horse ever to race around the State Fair track was Dan Patch, a pacer. He appeared in 1904, and while he didn't break world record, he did set a new State Fair record.

OTHER RACES

In 1923, mules ridden by well-known newspaper men and public officials raced. (Well, they sort of raced.)

DAN PATCH 1:55¼

THE FASTEST HARNESS HORSE THE WORLD HAS EVER SEEN.

DAN PATCH 1:55¼ IS OWNED BY INTERNATIONAL STOCK FOOD CO., MINNEAPOLIS, MINN., U. S. A.

That's the same year the Methodist Women's Society conducted a mail-in campaign protesting the sale of beer at the Fair, but the City Council issued five beer permits anyway. Twenty years later, you could buy a beer at the Fair on Sunday.

The cowboy who drew the largest crowds at the Fair was Roy Rogers, in 1956 and again in '59. But by the 1970s, cowboys and rodeos were being replaced by "big name" entertainment. Even so, rodeos still remain a small part of the State Fair venue, unlike those nighttime pageants that exploded during the '20s. Alas, the pageants are history—and what a shame. Everybody should get to see at least one!

Take the Fall of Troy, a highlight of the 1927 Fair. First, vaudeville acts warmed up the crowd. Then, as brass bands played popular tunes and "plump, graceful ladies in pink furbelows pranced along tight wires under dazzling arches," somebody stoked up the gunpowder, and Troy was detonated. Pyrotechnics produced all sorts of mayhem, from the "barbarism" of the Germans in World War I to the Spirit Lake Massacre.

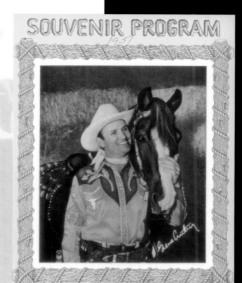

Sometimes, the point was to destroy a civilization, although never a Western one. Other times, the point was to portray history, although not accurately. No matter—the show always closed with a fireworks display of the American flag. Grand as all this was, by the 1930s, Iowans decided that pageants looked better in the movie theatre, and the big shows fizzled out. Happily, though, magnificent fireworks still light up the night skies after every Grandstand concert.

113

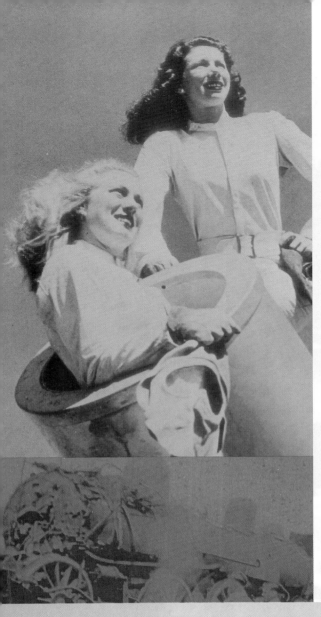

Then, There Were Trains...

Thrill shows, European and American circus acts and big bands replaced the pageants. Perhaps no thrill shows were as curious as the collisions—so bizarre that today no insurance company in the world would underwrite them!

One of the colossal collisions occurred on a rainy day in 1932. Forty-five thousand people and national news reel companies gathered to see a head-on crash between two 112-ton locomotives that had been destined for the junkyard. The turnout was especially high, considering that striking farmers seeking higher prices were picketing roads. The two locomotives, each pulling a tender, were named Hoover and Roosevelt in honor of the upcoming election. They faced off on a 3,000-foot track that was inclined at each end to enable the engines to pick up speed. Their couplings were primed with dynamite, and their coaches hauled lighted torches poised next to open cans of gasoline.

First, the engineers climbed aboard, fired up the engines, headed down the incline and began picking up speed!

And then?

And then the engineers jumped out!

And then?

The engines crashed into each other, hurling metal and wood debris in all directions, jarring the entire fairgrounds, creating huge clouds of black smoke and injuring two spectators.

Everything except the injuries was what promoter Joseph S. Connolly had promised. (He spoke from experience, staging similar crashes at the Iowa State Fair in 1896 and 1921.)

1906

116

PLANES...

By the turn of the century, fairgoers were fixed on aviation! Each day of the 1906 Fair, a sausage-shaped airship, powered by a five-horsepower engine, lifted off from the fairgrounds, circled the State Capitol and returned. One account said that "men refused to believe their eyes and children stood in amazement." Five years later, the Wright biplane caused a buzz. Many fairgoers had never seen a plane before, and now, here were these great birds creating figure 8s and going up and down at the will of the operator. By the time the 1911 Fair wrapped up, the board decreed: "...the aeroplane is to play a tremendous part in the civilization of the future. With the growth of aeroplane factories, peace commissions will go out of business. War will be simply impossible with these great birds of the air carrying high explosives and flying at will by daylight or in the dark of night over cities, fortifications and battleships. The enemy in the air will hold lives in the hollow of his hand."

In 1914, Lincoln Beachey and Eddie Rickenbacker, a famous racecar driver who later achieved fame as a pilot, faced off in a five-mile race around the track. Rickenbacker's Duesenberg was given a

Sincerely
Ruth Law

In 1908, when Amelia Earhart was living in Des Moines, her father took her to the Iowa State Fair to celebrate her 11th birthday. It was there that she saw her first airplane and reported that she was not impressed with the thing made of wood and rusty wire. She was impressed, however, with a funny hat made of a peach basket that she had purchased for 15 cents.

117

By the end of the 1930s, fairgoers had become so accustomed to mayhem that when stunt flyer Dick Granere's plane accidentally struck the ground injuring three spectators, **The Des Moines Register** *called it an "unscheduled airplane crash."*

handicap of one-half mile, and won by five seconds. Beachey, by the way, was flying a plane—sometimes at less than 10 feet above Rickenbacker. Another year, Ruth Law transferred from an auto to an airplane in flight. In 1928, fairgoers saw the Lockheed-Vega plane in which Capt. Sir George H. Wilkins and Lt. Carl Ben Eielson flew across the North Pole. In 1930, they met up with the Travelair Mystery Ship capable of speeds exceeding 300 mph. (Whew!) That same year, a barnstorming troupe—the Sons O Guns—collided over the northeast edge of the track. One plane crashed into the crowd, killing a Mitchellville man and injuring seven others. During the 1936 Fair, Roland Kumzaid strapped wings on his arms, jumped from a plane and flapped his way to the ground every afternoon.

But the wildest may have been in 1937: F.F. "Bowser" Frakes, a racecar driver who posed as a pilot, smashed a World War I Jenny biplane into a frame house that had been constructed in front of the Grandstand just so it could be destroyed. Before a crowd of 65,000, Frakes flew through the air, dipped down and rammed into the house. The impact tore off the wings, but the fuselage kept going, stopping 50 feet later. As the house burst into flames, an ambulance sped up to the plane, picked up a victim and darted away.

Ah, but the drama's not yet over! When the ambulance stopped outside the Grandstand, Frakes wasn't inside. He had slipped away—lucky for him, considering that deliberately crashing a plane (not to mention buzzing a crowd) was illegal. Authorities set up vigils at the Des Moines Airport to keep Frakes from taking off, but he flew out of a grain field east of the city.

Captain Frakes returned in 1950, crawled into a coffin and blew up seven sticks of dynamite. Afterward, he stood up and appeared to be a bit shaken and dazed. (No kidding!) The explosion left a sizable crater in the racetrack that had to be repaired before other events could take place.

Then, there was Ramon LaRue. In 1951, he put on a straitjacket, fastened his ankles to cables connected to a helicopter and was hauled up 300 feet. At that point, he escaped from his straitjacket, unshackled his feet, did a somersault and ended up swinging from a trapeze.

Captain Frakes and Mr. LaRue aside, wild and wooly plane shows became obsolete after World War II. In the 1960s, you could view the Fair from a helicopter, until one pilot lost control and made an unscheduled landing on East 30th and Des Moines streets. From then on, about the only "air show" was somebody spraying the grounds with insecticide prior to opening day.

So fairgoers shifted their attention to displays—a U.S. Air Force F-84E Thunderjet Fighter (partly produced by the Solar Aircraft Company in Des Moines); battle-tested weapons from Korea, a "snorkel jeep" that operated in water; rockets used by State University of Iowa scientists, including Dr. James Van Allen, to explore space more than 50 miles above the earth; a cut-through display of a Navy Phantom jet; a space suit; helicopter rockets—all kinds of machines that tripped the imagination.

Obviously, those attractions change with the times. And while they're interesting, you have to admit that they're pretty tame compared with those thrill shows. But that's what happens when Federal Aviation Administration regulations prohibit pilots from dive-bombing into a house while thousands watch from the Grandstand.

...AND AUTOMOBILES

Automobiles showed up for their first State Fair race in 1911. That year, Ray Harroun, winner of the 500 Mile Motor Car Contest on the Indianapolis Speedway, and Wild Bob Burman, who had traveled faster over the ground for one mile than anyone else in the history of the world, teamed up in a car. (One drove and the other manually pumped oil into the engine.) They were to race some planes, but after waiting 25 minutes for the signal to begin, the pilots landed and refused to go up again. In 1917, one person drove your basic Model T frame (plus an engine) while a polo player in the right-hand seat reached out to hit the ball with his mallet. Appropriately, this was called auto polo.

But it was those open-wheel sprint cars back in the late 1920s that so hooked Iowans (SO hooked them, in fact, that today, auto racing is the largest spectator sport in the state). Thousands packed into the Grandstand—not just during the Fair but throughout the whole racing season—to watch drivers reach speeds of 60 to 70 miles per hour. If the track was muddy, their nobbies (tires with cleats) dug in, picked

123

up dirt and threw it 50 feet as the cars careened around curves. Spectators were plastered with mud, but hey—this is racing!

The sport took a hiatus during World War II when gas and tires were in short supply. Afterward, street stock ruled, with drivers branching into different classes—cars with a two-barrel or four-barrel carburetor and one with this tire, another with that. By the 1950s, folks were filling up the Grandstand to watch Jimmie Lynch's Death Dodgers, Hollywood daredevil Joie Chitwood and Art Swenson's Slide for Life. One of his "sliders" was Ted Devlin of Des Moines. Ted's job was to:

1. ride on the rear bumper of a car going 60 miles an hour,

2. drop off the car when it reached a flaming pool of gasoline, and

3. slide through the fire.

Mr. Devlin was in good company. Stunt drivers in cars collided head-on, catapulted through the air, crashed into a pile of cars, soared from one ramp to another or roared around "Roman-style." (That's when the driver pilots the car from the roof top, rather than behind the wheel.) During the mid-'80s, monster trucks lurched onto the track, jumping cars and earth berms and creating noises that can cause an entire audience to collectively shake!

The sport of pulling goes back to the early days of the 20th century, with draft horse pulling. The first recorded "motorized" event took place in 1929 at Bowling Green, Missouri, but pulling really caught on in the '50s and '60s. In 1968, Iowa was one of a handful of Midwestern states to hold the first-ever tractor pulls.

We're told the sport originated when one guy told another guy that his tractor could pull more weight. Whether that's true or not, the contest remains the same. Drivers pull mechanical sleds behind either trucks or tractors. Some drivers in the '70s and '80s pulled with regular old garden tractors. But the real thrill is provided by drivers who climb aboard behemoth smoke-belching, earth-shaking, ear-shattering tractors—modified tractors, super modified tractors with dragster motors—you get the picture. Then, each tractor pulls a sled bearing anywhere from 5,000 to 60,000 pounds for up to 300 feet. The one who goes the farthest is the winner. (We think this sounds easier than it really is!)

The granddaddy of 'em all is Robbie Knievel, who hopped on his motorcycle in 1998, revved up, took off and jumped over 15 Kenworth semi-trailer trucks lined up on the Grand Concourse. Dad Evel's record was 13—proof that people may not be getting saner but they're getting better at doing crazy things.

By now that half-mile track in front of the Grandstand has seen it all—sprint cars, stock cars, midgets, big cars, jalopies, hot rods, coupes, sedans, late models and super modifieds…driven by Bunny Thornton, Gus Schrader, Emory Collins, Jimmy Wilburn, Barney Oldfield, Johnny Beauchamp, Eddie Anderson, Deb Snyder, Frank Luptow, Bill Holland, Leon DeRock.

By now, too, almost anything goes as far as engines are concerned. And that can produce Very Loud Noises! (Late models roar at 100 mph; sprint cars scream at 135 mph.) By the 1970s, noise was becoming a real issue with the fairgrounds' unhappy neighbors, some of whom wanted the racing season cancelled—not a good thing, considering the Des Moines State Fair Speedway was the largest track in Iowa. Finally, in 1979, the Iowa State Fairgrounds Racing Committee announced that cars must have a cast iron exhaust manifold, mufflers and a two-barrel carburetor, which apparently quiets things down. A State Fair report praised the decision, saying, "We commend George Barton and the members of the Iowa State Fairgrounds Racing Committee on making this just decision before some legislator in the State House came up with something worse."

COMING HOME

LeGrande Pinckney of Des Moines was a mechanic, truck driver, auto racing fan and—eventually—a race car driver himself. In 1951, he won the State Fair Championship in his '34 Ford coupe. His sons say winning that was a very big deal for him.

Mr. Pinckney quit racing in 1979 but came back 11 years later for the Old Timers' Race during the summer season. He ended the race upside down in his car. So he retired again.

But LeGrande Pinckney returned one last time.

It was that same year, after his funeral and cremation. One evening, four of his five sons were driving around trying to decide what to do with the ashes, when they came past the Fairgrounds. The turning gate just happened to be open…

Parking the car, the men walked onto the track their father had loved for so long. And in the dusk of evening, they spread his cremains from the fourth corner past the flag stand. Beyond them, someone was grading the track, and although that person never knew it, he helped Mr. Pinckney on his final journey home.

IOWA
STATE
FAIR
AUG. 23
~ SEPT. 1

GIVE US THAT OLD-TIME ROCK 'N' ROLL!

He prances out on stage, swaggering around while the music blares behind him and the Grandstand crowd roars approval. He hasn't sung a note yet. No matter! He showed up, didn't he? And he's wearing those skin-tight pants and that bright yellow jacket which he might or might not take off before everything's over.

"Lou! Lou! Lou! Lou!" they're chanting now, BIC lighters peppering the darkness as Lou Christie gets ready to yowl!

It's yet another Rock 'n' Roll Reunion. For the audience, if it's just like the last Rock 'n' Roll Reunion, that'll be okay! It's the sameness that counts.

So, where'd all this start? Well, back in 1980, Fair officials still had a couple of nights of entertainment to book for the Grandstand when somebody suggested a reunion of folksingers. Others didn't think that sounded as exciting as a reunion of rock 'n' roll singers. So Bill Fisher, the Fair's assistant manager at the time; Phil Webb, then the advertising agency account executive; Dic Youngs, KIOA-Oldies 93.3 disc jockey forever; and a Los Angeles disc jockey who was "connected" pulled together the lineup— Jimmie Rodgers, The Association, Bobby Vee, Del Shannon, Freddie (Boom-Boom) Cannon, Lesley Gore and the Marvelettes.

(Mr. Christie wasn't part of that year, but he hasn't missed many since.)

Twenty-five hundred people rocked that first year. Five thousand rocked the second year of what has now become ritual. Mr. Youngs emcees. ("They hired me to do this," he says, "but I would have done that first one for free!") People dance in the aisles and do the Locomotion on the stairs. They clap and stomp and sing themselves hoarse. It doesn't matter who the headliner is. Nor does it matter if the evening is cold and rainy or humid beyond belief. Folks still meet ahead of time—some in groups with matching T-shirts—at the Bud Tent, where the party starts about 5:30 P.M. every year.

Lesley Gore

COASTERS

LOU CHRISTIE

THE MARVELOUS MIDWAY

Some of us have the Midway memorized. We know where the Double Ferris Wheel and Guess Your Age and Weight game will be located every year. We watch youngsters spy the Submarine Ride before their parents know what's going on. We turn queasy as teen-agers climb into the Windshear, twirl around and upside down, stagger off and race back to do it again. We might admit that the Midway is crowded, loud and gaudy. But for goodness sake, that's what a Midway is *supposed* to be! If you want quiet, go watch them judge gladioluses.

Others of us know the Midway is "over there"—north of the Grand Concourse and east of the Grandstand. But we haven't walked through it for decades. Our stomach can't take the Tilt-a-Whirl, and we couldn't win a big fuzzy bear if the operator let us stand inside the rope to pitch those coins. The Midway is way too crowded, way too loud and way too gaudy to ever lure us in. But we wouldn't want it to disappear. Because the Midway is as much a part of the State Fair as are the Cattle Barn and the corn dog.

It wasn't always so, of course. In the beginning, the ISAS believed that if something wasn't educational, it shouldn't be part of the Fair. So George W. DeHaven's Great Union Circus and J.A. Bailey's Grand International Menagerie,

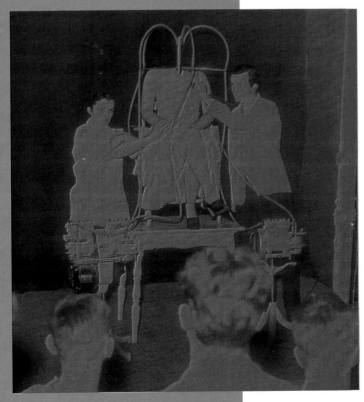

Museum, Aquarium and Circus had to set up outside the fair-grounds fence. By the mid-1880s, quality sideshows that were "not particularly elevating but not reprehensible" were invited to set up on the grounds.

Well, wouldn't you just know—some less-than-quality acts worked their way in too. Games like chuck-a-luck (played with three dice), fortune-tellers and men in checkerboard suits with valises full of Punch and Judy whistles roamed the grounds. The sleazier sideshows and dancing girls remained on the perimeter.

Wallaces Farmer, among others, did not approve, suggesting that the Midway "be done away with, and the stream of filth which flows from it should be dammed up once and for all." Instead, the Fair Board hired landscape architect O.C. Simonds in 1910 to draw a plan that confined the amusements to an area just east of the Grandstand.

That way, they wouldn't disturb people who came to enjoy the Fair but not to see a sideshow. And so, our Midway was born.

Like everything else, the Midway keeps evolving. Gone are the barkers—those guys who used a megaphone or a microphone or just a God-given, really loud voice to "bark" about all sorts of oddities from freak shows to fun houses. The noise levels the men reached as they tried to over-ride one another got to be too much even for a midway, and the practice was discontinued.

137

Also, there used to be "kiddy" and "major" rides. Now, there are "spectacular" rides as well. Back in the 1980s, the Mighty Bluegrass Shows could purchase a kiddy ride for $5,000 and a spectacular ride for $100,000. Today, kiddy rides cost $100,000; spectacular rides cost $1 million. Plus, the ride and game operators of old now are technicians who use computers.

Bottom line as far as the Midway is concerned? Safe rides, fair games. Every year, the Iowa Department of Inspections and Appeals, the Attorney General's Office, the Division of Criminal Investigation

and the Iowa State Patrol check—among other things—the diameter and shape of basketball hoops, the rebound slope of ball-tossing games and the inflation in basketballs. The games just have to be winnable, not easily winnable, say law enforcement officials.

Consequently, in 1997, one basketball game worker had to remove large stuffed animals hanging along the front of the booth because they interfered with players' shots. Another had to take air out of over-inflated basketballs and put up a sign telling players the hoops were not regulation size. A dart game operator had to display the winning numbers instead of hiding them behind his balloons. Why? Seems certain partially hidden numbers looked so much the same that the operator could decide whether the winning number was a "1" and you got a plastic comb or a "7" and you got a three-foot panda.

Even if you don't go near a game, parting with money has never been a problem. People have paid to see a rose-colored horse (the rose was white) or a horse with his head where his tail ought to be (the animal was turned around in the stall), or to learn how to whittle (use the blade away from yourself).

THE STATE FAIR ROLLER COASTER

Some people somewhere in Des Moines are living in houses built from a wooden roller coaster.

The roller coaster was constructed in 1908 northeast of the Grandstand (now a parking lot) and was owned by Jimmie and Johnny Kenenan of Oklahoma City. Before the Fair resumed in 1946—after a four-year hiatus because of World War II—the decision was made to tear down the coaster because it was rotting around the footings. Materials were in short supply, so that spring, former Fair Secretary A. R. Corey's two sons (along with 12 other men) dismantled the coaster and sold the lumber to a carpenter for construction of houses.

According to an article in *The Des Moines Register*, "To the hardened roller coaster addict, the Fair ride was tamer than those at Arnolds Park or Riverview in Des Moines. But tens of thousands of others found it plenty exciting."

One of those others was Fair Secretary Lloyd Cunningham's grandfather, Jasper. Jasper went on the wild ride with his grandson sometime before 1915. Afterwards, another member of the Cunningham family put Grandpa's experience into verse:

"Up and down, round and round,
*   then came the dip of death,*
Granddad, cussing like a trooper,
*   when he could get his breath,*
At last it stopped and Jasper said,
*   "Let's sit down in the shade;*
That dum [sic] thing made me dizzy
*   and I'll buy some lemonade."*

GOOD GRIEF! GIRLIE SHOWS!

For Iowa kids wandering the Midway, nothing tantalized so much as the notion that a whole lot of sinning was going on inside that tent where the girls were dancing. You couldn't go in, of course. Or at least, you weren't supposed to. But that didn't stop you from imagining!

Some say the images conjured up probably were more risqué than the real thing. But alas, we'll not know because the girls are gone—replaced by movies and television. Still, for the better part of a century—beginning in the 1890s—those young ladies were part of the Fair. In fact, by the turn of the century, the Iowa State Fair had a reputation among midway operators for being a good place to set up girlie shows. The first striptease acts appeared in the early '30s, and by 1935, girls were reported to be dancing around stark naked. At least that's what Gus Alesch heard. So, the State Legislator listened to the pitch outside the tent, noting that the barker promised girls would perform in the buff. To confirm the barker's honesty, Mr. Alesch went inside.

The barker's word was good as gold. According to the lawmaker, "Not so much as a piece of corn plaster interposed itself between the goggle-eyed public and the girls' epidermis . . . If the same thing happens at the next Fair, I think I can get a number of clean-minded men to go out and clean it up with a club."

Mr. Alesch should have sat closer to the stage. Although the girls seemed to be dancing in the nude, they were cleverly clothed in tights that appeared to be bare skin in the purposefully dim light.

(Another time, dancers wore only cellophane. Alas, the cellophane was black, not clear. But you had to pay admission to find that out.)

Probably the highlight occurred in 1947 when Sally Rand blew into town. By day, she lived in her own circus van, decorated by a New York firm and fitted with a private telephone and air conditioning. By night, she packed 'em in on the Midway. Folks were intent on seeing what there was to see beyond those slow-moving ostrich plume fans. She attracted such large audiences that the Grandstand filled up more slowly than usual, causing fairgoers to miss at least part of the State Fair Revue of "Tally Ho," featuring ballet dancers dressed in dashing red-flecked riding costumes.

Miss Rand was no doubt the most famous gal to bump and grind her way around the Midway. But we must also mention Evelyn West, the girl with the "$100,000 Treasure Chest," who walked back and forth across the outside stage while a barker embellished on her accomplishments and indicated there was much more to be seen after you paid your admission and went inside. And Denise Darnell, a 6-foot, 6-inch performer billed as the world's tallest showgirl.

THIS IS AN
UNFINISHED PROO...

So Much Entertainment, So Little Time

Over the years, there has been so much going on at the Iowa State Fair that a person could skip the Grandstand and the Midway and still be entertained day and night…

…by performers on Bill Riley, Walnut, American Republic, Fairview, Grand Concourse, Miller and Fun Forest Stages…

…by the Toby Show; some fellow who puts on his lederhosen once a year and plays an accordion up on the hill; or furry little creatures in the Petting Zoo…

…by spectacular Dancing Waters; Paul Munsen's mystifying magic; or acrobats who look like Laurel and Hardy…

…by Brian Ruth's animal sculptures created from tree stumps and a very loud chain saw; Russ Burgess hypnotizing people; or the Comedy Chimps…

…by 50 tons of sticky sand molded into a castle 16 feet tall; the Mitchell Marionettes; or the next batch of presidential hopefuls stumping their way across Iowa…

Or maybe, all the entertainment you'll need can be provided by Duffy Lyon. Her story starts in 1960, but we're going clear back to 1911. That was the first year the Fair initiated an annual exhibit to promote dairy products: a cow sculpted out of butter. In 1956, when a new sculptor presented his first cow, Ms. Lyon was critical. "It was a lousy cow," said the woman, who had taken a sculpting class at Iowa State.

Four years later, the job was hers. So the farmwife from Toledo and niece of State Fair author Phil Stong, began sculpting her own 600-pound cows.

Lettie Martens of Gilmore City was absolutely determined that her granddaughter, Denise Shipler of Burt, would perform in the annual Governor's Very Special Arts Festival. The Festival, one of the Fair's free stage shows, is sponsored by Very Special Arts Iowa. "You really ought to hear my granddaughter sing," she kept suggesting to Festival director Gwen Burke. In fact, she suggested it so many times that Ms. Burke says, "Finally, in 1986 we took a chance and put Denise on the Concourse Stage in front of an audience of 1,200. Because we'd never heard her sing before, we sandwiched her in between two acts that we knew were big draws."

And so Ms. Shipler, who was born *without* any arms and one leg but *with* an absolutely beautiful voice, took the stage with her pianist and drummer, sang "Operator," and brought the house down. Someone from the Variety Club of Iowa was in the audience and—well, you know how those success stories go. Since then, Ms. Shipler has performed throughout the United States, Canada and Australia, often with Variety Club International; she's cut two gospel albums and has a single featuring "The Iowa Song"; and she has appeared on the Variety Club of Iowa Telethon every year since 1987. And you lucky ones can say, "Hey, I saw that young lady way back when—at the Iowa State Fair!"

She works in a 40-degree refrigerated showcase in the Agriculture Building, swathing butter across a wood and steel frame, then carving by hand. Twenty-five years into carving cows, she expanded her repertoire to include the likes of Grant Wood's American Gothic, Garth Brooks and Smokey the Bear. But the biggies have been a six-foot Elvis, which caused U.S. Secretary of Agriculture Dan Glickman to remark, "My heart started to beat fast when I saw him," and the Last Supper, which caused Ms. Lyon's assistant, Ruth Nixt, to remark, "One of the Apostles down at the end of the table looked a little like my brother-in-law."

Every year, thousands wait patiently to file by the display case. The line—sometimes 20 deep—stretches past the ice sculptures, the Iowa Turkey Federation exhibit and the Iowa Egg Council booth, which is already congested because they're giving away samples of cherry crepes.

And that, friends, is how
Iowans entertain themselves at the Fair!

THE AG EXTRAVAGANZA OF IOWA

"Most of the farmers who come to the Fair come there because the don't intend to get lef behind. They want to know the last word i up-to-date machinery and improved livestoc but they expect to get their best information from their fellow farmers whom they meet at the Fair."

Henry A. Wallace
September 10, 1926

Some people go to the Fair and don't take in anything even remotely connected with agriculture. Oh, my! Are they missing a lot! Where else can you see Big Daddy, a Duroc purebred boar that weighs 1,062 pounds? Or watch bees make honey while you're eating honey? Or clap for Champions on Parade?

Whether you live on a farm or occasionally drive by one, you ought to take in the agricultural side of the Fair. Agriculture, after all, is why the Iowa State Agricultural Society established an annual exposition. The event was to be a simple showcase, primarily of stock and grains. Farmers would exchange experiences, discuss breeds of animals, types of grains, the latest inventions and rotation systems, and compete for ribbons showing "meritorious exertion." More than anything else, the Fair would be a three-day school experience focusing on livestock, produce and machinery.

RISK

ALL THOSE ANIMALS DOWN ON THE FARM

The first day of the first Fair was devoted to showing stock. *The Fairfield Ledger* later wrote, "We doubt whether any State Fair in the Union ever had a finer display of choice stock at their first State Fair… [It had] horses, cattle, mules, sheep and hogs." Even so, few if any diplomas were awarded for livestock, probably because the judges weren't sure they were observing the best quality of animals Iowans owned.

Two years later, at the 1856 Fair in Muscatine, a reporter for *The St. Louis Democrat* decided the problem might not be with the quality of the animals as with the quality of the farmers:

"There was a large collection of very fair stock exhibited, but little strictly choice. Carelessness was noticeable throughout, and we were disposed to attribute the defect more to the mode of keeping than inferiority of breeds. The farmers of Iowa have not given sufficient attention, we fear, to the manner of feeding and raising stock—in brief, they do not, as a class, fully appreciate the advantages of high-toned agricultural periodicals and works on the same subject. Exceptions can, of course, be found, and these few exceptions do more good in the community than 10 dozen old-fashioned farmers who will neither make improvements themselves nor adopt those of others."

Certainly, farmers weren't as smart as they are now. For example, in the mid-1800s, they believed the fatter the cow, the better the animal. An early premium list informed potential exhibitors that "all other things being equal, those are the best cattle that have the greatest weight in the smallest superficies." Accordingly, fat cows were the winners. But in 1873, Adonijah Strong Welch, president of Iowa State College of Agriculture and Mechanic Arts, asked the Society to rethink rewarding the fatted calf, saying excessively fat stock was undesirable. Mr. Welch believed that the Society's policy forced farmers to raise some cattle to show and others to sell, which made the Fair a "museum of curiosities."

152

Thanks to competition and education via the annual State Fair, breeders began to see the importance of raising purebred stock that would either produce more milk or better beef. Shorthorns were a favorite because they furnished milk as well as beef. Other breeds were brought into the state over the years, and Iowa is now consistently ranked among the top 10 cattle-producing states.

153

But perhaps the real problem was with unqualified judges, rather than with the farmers or the animals. Nowhere was the issue of quality judges as acute as in livestock competition, where exhibitors had the most to gain in premiums and the prestige of winning at the Iowa State Fair. *The Iowa Homestead* complained, "Breeders are made to smart under the rod held over their heads by committee men [judges] who are not in any sense competent to do justice to so important an interest. Many an animal goes home with a commercial value much less than when it enters the grounds…[being] beaten in the ring by a beast not representing a fourth of its value." (continued on p.158)

So, what have fairgoers seen over the years? Here's a smattering of the livestock:

1859 There were 20 Devon, 29 Shorthorns, no Herefords or Alderneys, and only two milk cows. "[T]he best, that of J.N. Miller, was scarcely first rate, and the other ought to be called third rate. It is hoped that next year, at least 20 farmers' wives will each send a cow as well as specimens of butter."

1887 Standard-bred Trotters, Roadsters, Cleveland Bays, Clydesdales, French Draft, English and Canadian horses each had "peculiar excellencies."

1923 Of the 750 head of sheep, 61 lambs were shown by Iowa boys and girls. There were also 32 milk goats shown by three exhibitors. More than $105,000 was paid out in cash premiums for stock, one of the largest sums paid out by any Fair in the country.

1970 A Holstein owned by Fred Hall of Fort Dodge won the first Moo-la Sweepstakes. Not just a beauty contest, these cows are judged on pounds of milk produced and number of calves born.

1999 Ten sows farrowed during the Fair. Crowds passed along an elevated walkway by the farrowing crates while Kirkwood Community College students answered questions and held up the 104 baby pigs. (Yes, city folks asked when the little white pigs would turn black and white.)

Iowa State's Welch began pushing for competition based on uniform standards and the use of knowledgeable judges (often professors). Today, qualified judges help point breeders and exhibitors in the right direction; their public selection of champions signals what kind of animal should be raised.

By the early 1900s, the Fair had shifted from being a "school" where Iowans learned how to improve products through competition to learning from outside experts. Iowa State students and graduates taught new farming ideas, techniques and practices at the Fair. Over the years, educational and support organizations, community colleges, universities, extension services, county agricultural societies and state and federal agencies also served as clearinghouses of information. Today, the Fair is unsurpassed in livestock, having been first to:

• have a beef carcass show and a lamb carcass evaluation;

• hold attitude and appearance contests for swine exhibitors;

• weigh breeding beef cattle as they enter the show ring;

• provide the judge with all production data;

• have 4-H production classes and other showing improvements; and

• require butchering of some grand champion animals for meat-type evaluation.

HANGING THE JUDGE

August 7, 1888
TO: Hiram C. Wheeler, ESQ, President, Iowa State Agriculture Society, Odebolt, Iowa
FROM: Burgess Brothers of Wenona, Illinois

Dear Sir:

On January 30, 1888, we received [a letter from Fair Secretary Shaffer] saying he was instructed by the Board to forward us a copy of a resolution…prohibiting us from hereafter showing [our horses] on the grounds of your Society.

Now, I can assure you and the Board that we were entirely ignorant at the time of who the parties were that hung the [horse competition] judge in effigy.

Now, it does seem unfair to accuse and convict us of something we were entirely innocent of without even giving us a hearing…We have attended a large number of the leading fairs of this country in the last five years, have always aimed to make a choice exhibit and do our best for the interest of the different societies and for the Shire horse…[G]ive us a hearing before the board some time during the coming fair, and if we fail to make it satisfactory we are willing to refund the Society our last year's premiums, and also the premiums of this year, should we be lucky enough to win any.

THE OPEN CLASS LIVESTOCK SHOW

The heart of an agriculture fair is the Open Class Livestock Show. Here, purebred breeders show off their best as judges pace, poke and prod while considering which animal sports the best breeding or market qualities. Thousands stay for hours to see their favorite breed, to note who is raising what or to discern changes in the industry. Before they go back home, some of those thousands will buy. But all of them will know more than they did before coming to the Fair. Guaranteed.

For more than a century, the livestock shows have earned the Iowa State Fair a national reputation of excellence.

Still, even shows that have enjoyed a run this long constantly change. For example, it used to be the livestock showed up before the Fair started and stuck around until the end. Now, there isn't room to house all the animals at once. And, quite frankly, breeders today don't have the luxury of spending 11 days at the Fair. So animals come and go. For

instance, FFA sheep and wool breeds fill up the stalls those first four days of the Fair; then come the 4-H sheep, followed by the meat breeds.

Used to be, too, that the owners spent their nights in the barn. In fact, until 1986, sheep exhibitors slept in the loft, and some still sleep in the pen. Competition also used to include colored-wool (red, black and white) sheep, but that's been discontinued.

As long as we're talking sheep, all the action isn't in the show ring. The first Saturday of the Fair, the Stewart Sunbeam Oster Co. of McMinnville, Tennessee, sponsors a shearing contest. Between 200 and 250 sheep get very quick haircuts (okay, wool-cuts). In his day, it took Charlie Swaim from Drakesville between 90 seconds and three minutes to shear a sheep. "It's a little bit technique and a little bit the luck of the draw," Mr. Swaim says. "Certain sheep are easier to shear." Judges consider speed, number of cuts made (ouch!) and the severity of those cuts. Mr. Swaim won four national championships. (He doesn't remember how many state championships he brought home.) But then, he had lots of practice shearing about 25,000 sheep a year at packing plants.

THE BIG BULL

JC Mac Stud competed only in the 1995 World's Super Bull contest. But once was enough. The Angus took first place that year, and no bull before or since has come close to his 3,360 pounds.

Thing was, his owner, Jerry Carrico of Carrico Angus Farm in Redfield says if his bull had cooperated, he would have weighed even more. The family had been watching this "tremendously big-framed bull," and in the spring of '95, put him on a set of farm scales; he weighed 3,560 pounds. Mr. Carrico thought, "Wow!" then wondered if the scales were correct. So he hauled JC Mac Stud to town, led him across the local coop scales and thought "Wow!" again. By Fair time, the bull was down to 3,450 because of the heat.

JC Mac Stud had been to the Fair before— in 1989, he and his dam were cow-calf champions, and he was junior bull calf champion; in 1990, he was reserve junior champion; in 1991, he was reserve senior champion. Still, he didn't particularly like the Fair. And on this particular day in 1995, he had to stay in his stall from 9 a.m. until weigh-in at 6 p.m., which he also didn't like. Just before the competition began, he ate a bit, but wouldn't drink.

Weigh-in was tense. The old record weight was 3,258 pounds, and Jumbo #2, a Charolais belonging to Joe Holub of What Cheer, broke that record by two pounds. But then JC Mac Stud broke Jumbo #2's record by 100 pounds!

Afterward, Mr. Carrico took JC Mac Stud to the tie-out area, where he drank three five-gallon pails of water—thereby upping his weight by another 120 pounds.

The bull grazed around the farm for another year, mostly for sentimental reasons, but when he became arthritic, the family decided to ship him to market. It was difficult to find a slaughterhouse set up to handle an animal that size.

VERY LARGE ANIMALS

Each year, big boars, bulls and rams weigh in at the Fair, and the heaviest in each category wins an 11-day stay. Here's a look at three mighty meaty fellows.

The Largest Horse Contest ran from 1991 through 1997. Lumbering home with first-place honors were Doc, Tom, Tim, Big Red, Blondie, Golitha and Tony. Trust us, they were very big horses.

THE BIG RAM

The first time Daryl and Jason Mickelson of Perry saw the ram at Lizer's Livestock Auction, Inc., in Gowrie, he was thin and had obviously not been taken care of. Although the Mickelsons noted his absolutely huge frame, dad Daryl thought the sheep wouldn't live; son Jason thought the sheep could be a contender in the Big Ram Contest. So that day in 1997, the Suffolk left Gowrie with the Mickelsons. Young Mr. Mickelson was working for Gustafson, Inc., in Redfield, so they named the big ram Gus.

It took time to nurse Gus back to good health. The Mickelsons began feeding Gus a pellet feed and corn mixture, slowly working him up to eight pounds a day. When the '98 Fair arrived, Jason gave Gus a bath, via the garden hose and soap. "It took lots of scrubbing," Jason recalls, "but he loved the attention." Cleaned-up Gus weighed in at 464 pounds—30 pounds

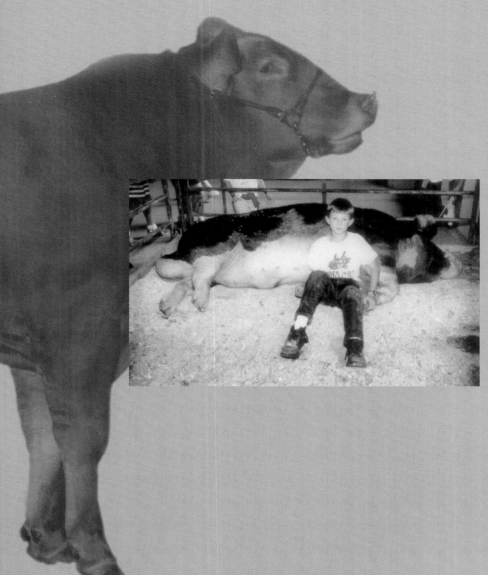

THE BIG BOAR

Big John was appropriately named. At 1,004 pounds, the purebred black Poland China was the biggest boar at the 1977 State Fair. Two years later and two pounds heavier (if that's possible), he was again named the biggest boar.

Big boars prepare for competition by eating; otherwise, they'd only weigh 700 or 750 pounds. "And they eat well," says Harlan Hirsch of Hirsch Farms, Ltd., in Indianola, whose boars—Big John, Zachariah, Commander, Big Daddy, Commando and Apollo—have eaten their way to first place seven times since the inaugural competition in 1975. "They have to be good on their feet and legs or they can't carry the weight," he says.

Winners lounge beneath a fan in the northwest corner of the Swine Barn, as thousands file by, pausing to gaggle and gasp at the immense amount of pork. Afterward, some boars are used for breeding. Zachariah, Mr. Hirsch's 1,062-pound purebred Duroc, who waddled off with first place in 1989, was purchased by Swine Genetics International, Ltd., in Cambridge. Others were sold to market. "If I'd have listened to the family, all our boars would still be here at home," Mr. Hirsch says. "But for practical and economic reasons, I just can't do that."

Truly, fame is fleeting.

more than any ram had ever weighed. The next year, Gus beat his own record by 15 pounds.

Gus was as nice as he was big. In his youth, he'd been a show ram, so he was used to being handled. Jason let kids go into his pen in the Sheep Barn to pet him. "He was kind of like an interactive display," says Jason. "I'd take him for walks, and kids would climb on for a ride. Lots of people came to the barn the second year at the Fair because they'd heard about Gus."

There was to be a third time at the Fair—maybe even a fourth. But a month after Gus earned his second championship, he became trapped in a piece of parked farm machinery and died. "A part of our family died with him," Jason says. "He was an incredible sheep who had a place at our farm for as long as he was alive. We hope everyone who met Gus enjoyed him as much as we did."

THE SALE OF CHAMPIONS

On the last Saturday of every Fair since 1988, some special kids and their special animals gather at 2 p.m. in the Penningroth Center in the Cattle Barn. They're joined by businesspeople, family, friends, members of the FFA and 4-H—plus an auctioneer—for the Sale of Champions. Sponsored by the Iowa Foundation for Agriculture Advancement, the event recognizes the best of the best as the Champion and Reserve Champion meat animals and poultry go to the highest bidders. Buyers must have the animals slaughtered at Iowa State University for educational purposes; all carcasses are graded and put on display in the meat lab at ISU. Then, the buyer can donate the meat back to the Foundation or to a charity, sell the meat or keep it. The Sale of Champions profits support Iowa youth livestock projects and a scholarship program.

RESERVE SR. CHAMPION
SHORTHORN FEMALE
IOWA STATE FAIR
1956

THE GOVERNOR'S CHARITY STEER SHOW

Look, out in the ring! It's Johnny Orr! No, it's Chubby Checker! Wrong again! It's Don Muhm!

Actually, at one time or another, you could have seen former Iowa State University basketball coach Johnny Orr or twister Chubby Checker or *Des Moines Register* farm editor Don Muhm in the Livestock Show Ring—each of them (carefully) leading a 1,200-pound steer through his paces at the Governor's Charity Steer Show. The show and auction, which began in 1983, has paired Iowa celebrities with some of the best-looking 4-H cattle to raise money for the state's three Ronald McDonald Houses. The show is sponsored by the Iowa Cattlemen's Association and the Iowa Beef Industry Council and hosted by the governor. Individuals, businesses and associations each purchase a steer (often, county fair winners), donate it for the auction, then choose a celebrity to show the animal. To date, their efforts have generated more than $815,000.

The project started off simply enough. A group of folks wanted to highlight Iowa's role in the beef industry. At that time, the World Steer Show was part of the Fair, so the Celebrity Steer Show was added. First host was former farm boy Terry Branstad, but he didn't show the winner. That was a steer sponsored by the Production Credit Association of Iowa and shown by Eric and Allison, the governor's children.

THE CELEBRITY SWINE SHOWMANSHIP CLASSIC

Since 1996, celebrities have paraded around with some fancy swine—celebrities like Governor Tom Vilsack* and Iowa State University President Martin Jischke and 1999 Fair Queen Abby Menke from Cherokee. Often with more courage than confidence, the celebrities enter the Swine Barn Show Ring with Yorkshires and Landraces and Chester Whites. Show sticks in hand, the celebrities "lead" their charges into and out of a swimming pool full of water, a farrowing crate tunnel and a flower garden, among other obstacles.

Sponsored by the Iowa Pork Producers Association and the Iowa Purebred Swine Council, the show's purpose is to have fun, which has not been a problem. Afterward, the MCs remind the audience to visit the Iowa Pork Tent. Appropriately!

*Dr. David Topel, ISU dean of agriculture, not the governor, took first place. However, Governor Vilsack did receive honorable mention PLUS a big hand from the crowd.

IN IOWA CORN IS KING

THE CROPS—FROM THE FIELD, FROM THE GARDEN

How fitting! The Agriculture Building anchors the middle of the Fairgrounds and resides at the heart of the Fair. Since 1904, the red brick building—with its exposition-style architecture—has probably enticed every fairgoer inside at least once. Who can pass up entering beneath that great rotunda? Who doesn't want to glide up the wide staircases? Who wouldn't take a turn around the oak balcony with its hardwood floors? And why wouldn't you find yourself a bench, plop down and watch all the folks who've come to look, to smell and (happily) to taste.

All That Horticulture at One End of the Building

It wouldn't be a State Fair without Agriculture Alley tables filled with produce like bright orange carrots (perfectly shaped—how do they do that?) and gallon jars of early barley and late oats. Plus, there are those strange-looking vegetables—like a tomato that's the spitting image of Bob Hope.

In Agriculture Alley, you can:

• remember the past. Certainly, the display of "old-time crops" set up by Dr. Wayne R. Hansen of Ames took folks back in time. Spotting one of the crops—flaxseed—caused one passerby to recall how fields of flax looked from a distance like a beautiful blue sea.

• peer into the future. The alley sports produce new to this state—Southern crops like okra and beet greens; Southeast Asian crops like bok choy and Oriental squash; Hispanic crops like hot peppers and nopales (that's cactus).

• mix the past with the future. Herbs have been around forever, but the everyday Iowan is now taking note of them. So Dr. Phil Levine from the Drake University College of Pharmacy & Health Sciences discusses the use of herbs for medicinal purposes.

But a trip through Agriculture Alley can also make you melancholy. The alley used to house 25 booths where families would exhibit their crops, tying the presentations into the Fair's theme. Today, there are three booths, and in 1999, only one was spoken for. That exhibit was by Darrell Besco of Chariton, his sisters Connie Thrasher of Des Moines and Sandy Besco of Berwick and nephew Justin Besco of Lucas. Darrell Besco has competed since 1962.

His exhibits feature grains and seed bundles, hay and almost anything you can grow in an Iowa garden—from plums to muskmelon. Sounds easy, but try finding six carrots that look alike. "You have to grow a lot of carrots to do that," Mr. Besco says. "Plus, you have to keep going back during the Fair to exchange new tomatoes, eggplants and cabbage for the old so everything looks fresh."

Still, he likes competing, as well as seeing people's reaction to the beauty of the produce. Mr. Besco and his family will keep coming back "until the category is phased out altogether" he says.

And All That Floriculture at the Other End of the Building

At the east end of the building, bask in the aroma of roses; learn to arrange dahlias or cornstalks; and find out not only how to grow herbs but also how to use them. You can't miss the gladiola competition since State Fair time is when they're flaunting those marvelous blooms. And you won't want to miss the table displays, with lush linens, fine china and bouquet centerpieces that tie all the colors and shapes together.

A floricultural highlight came in 1984, when the building's centerpiece was an 80-year-old burr oak tree—inside the building. The burr oak had spent its life on a Madison County Farm belonging to Jack and Florence Thomas. By '84, however, it was on

its last ring, and Dan Cooper—state horticulturalist with the Department of Agriculture and coordinator of the Ag Building—suggested it might make an interesting addition to the Fair. So the Thomases chopped down their tree, hauled it to Des Moines on a flatbed semitrailer truck, sawed off the limbs to get the tree inside the building, propped it up in a really big pot, tied it to the rafters with guy wires, then reattached the limbs by boring holes into the tree for connecting rods. Then, Dan Cooper, state horticulturist, decorated it with orchids.

The burr oak just made one appearance at the Fair, but the bees have been around forever. In the 1800s, beekeepers held annual meetings in a tent during the Fair. After World War II, a handful of beekeepers set up their first exhibit on the balcony. Today, the

172

A SWEET STORY

Folks line up at the Agriculture Building the last Friday of every Fair for the sweetest sweet corn in Iowa—made even better by the fact that it's free! And for that, we say thanks to Ron Deardorff.

Mr. Deardorff of Adel is a conventional farmer who also grows fresh market sweet corn. (It's available in most Des Moines-area Dahl's Food Marts and Hy-Vee Food Stores.) One day in 1995, some State Fair people decided that since Iowa is the [sweet] corn state, and since sweet corn is tastiest in August, the Fair should have a sweet corn feed. So they asked Mr. Deardorff to donate part of the 100 dozen ears needed. "I got to

thinking maybe I'd just donate all of it, and get some mileage out of the free advertising," Mr. Deardorff says. (Mr. Deardorff is an up-front man.)

On the last Thursday of every Fair, he gets up early, picks 1,200 ears of corn and delivers them to the Agriculture Building where they are shucked. The next day, somebody shows up with a big cooker and LOTS of water. At precisely 11 a.m., people who have been in line for a long time get sweet corn and some butter (but not from the butter cow), sit down on the grass by the Ag Building and eat.

Mr. Deardorff doesn't attend the feed; he's back in Adel, picking more corn.

beekeeper exhibit still attracts fairgoers like bees to...oh, never mind. The exhibit consists of about a dozen observation hives, each connected to a tunnel leading out of the building. The bees do the same thing they do back home—raise babies, collect water and nectar, make honey. Guard bees at each tunnel door make sure worker bees from neighboring observation hives don't come in. And somewhere amidst all of this are queen bees, laying eggs and raising young bees. (The queens are a bit larger and with a different coloration.) "The only problem with these bees," says Glen Stanley, who was superintendant of the honey and live bee exhibit from 1953 to 1988, "is they don't really like the light. Real hives are dark."

Even so, their hard work fascinates fairgoers. "I used to spend 12 hours a day during the Fair giving lectures to the crowds," says Mr. Stanley.

You can still sample some good Iowa honey, but the Meeting Place cafe on the balcony—which sold only Iowa food —is gone. Run by the National Council of Federated Garden Clubs of Iowa, the cafe opened in 1983. Until 1995, you could eat AE Cottage Cheese, a ham or turkey sandwich, gallons of coleslaw, apple dumplings, watermelons and muskmelons, and drink grape juice or cider, but not coffee or pop. Once when Mrs. Thomas brought in 100 dozen cinnamon rolls her sister had made, the Club wasn't going to serve them with coffee, that not being an Iowa product. But Mrs. Thomas wisely pointed out that you can't have cinnamon rolls without coffee.

Gomphrena

Water melon
Crimson Sweet

Beans
'Kidney'

Pumpkin
Jackpot

WHAT'S ON DISPLAY?

Here's a handful of the produce displayed over the years:

1859 Red African tea wheat was raised at the rate of 80 bushels per acre by planting it in drills and giving it extra attention. The heads and kernels were very large and long.

1887 Judges took into account grains, seeds and vegetables arranged in artistic style.

1921 "My father made me hoe and dig and fight weeds on our farm, and I didn't know what I was doing," recalls farm boy (and later WHO Radio farm director) Herb Plambeck. So he talked the Fair into launching a weed identification contest. Top prize was $3, which Mr. Plambeck won for three successive years.

1941 Lawrence Flander of Harper won the National Tall Corn Contest with a stalk that was 23 feet, 2¼ inches tall.

1983 Farmers entered their corn and soybeans in the first Iowa State Fair Open Market Quality Competition, a nutrient-analysis contest. Unlike beauty contests, these winners weren't always the best-looking crops.

1992 Jumbo vegetables set records: a 2.7-pound tomato, a 21.9-pound cabbage, a 47-pound pumpkin, a 412.5-pound squash, a 9.6-pound melon and a 70.7-pound watermelon.

"When I first started working at the Franklin Industries booth, people used to show up at 7:30 in the morning—farmers who already had chores done and were walking through. The times have changed. Now, the farmer crowd doesn't show up until 8:30 or 9. They're still farming, but they have jobs in town, too. They're trying to hold onto that farm. It's different today."

Ruhl Barker, sales representative of Franklin Industries, Inc.

NEW-FANGLED FARM MACHINERY

The ISAS believed Iowa must excel in manufacturing as well as agriculture. Consequently, manufacturing companies were invited to enter their products in Fair competition. Not surprisingly, most "products" were farming implements. And as with the best ear of corn or loaf of bread, the best implements were awarded cash prizes.

That changed in 1870 after the ISAS published a report, which included 50 pages of farm machinery illustrations. Because the report was paid for, in part, by a legislative appropriation, critics cried, "Foul!" claiming you can't use taxpayer money to promote implement dealers. The criticism was so stinging that the ISAS stopped awarding cash prizes to the implement dealers, since that cash also came from the Legislature. Instead, winners received

Farm implement displays have changed over the years, as you can see:

1859 A mole plow created concealed furrows used for draining land. In a day, two men could form an under-drain ditch from 50 to 100 rods, although the plow worked better with oxen.

1887 Until recently, all farm machinery, implements and tools were brought from abroad. By this time, however, many were being made here and could compete with the best European wares.

1906 Folks saw silage cutters that cut and elevated the corn into silos; 150 kinds of gasoline engines; a combined corn cutter/husker (which, alas, wasted the stalks); and a milking machine run by a gasoline engine which drew milk as well as anyone could by hand.

1924 Iowa State College's "manless plow" operated under its own power, with a man to guide it.

1965 J.I. Case Co. introduced the 1200 Traction King, a 4-wheel drive tractor that also featured 4-wheel steering. Unlike the others, the Traction King did not articulate—which means it didn't bend in the middle.

1999 Still popular after all these years (well, at least since the 1970s) were the Kane Manufacturing, Inc., heat mats, which made pig births less stressful. Baby pigs coming from a 102-degree womb were placed on heat mats in the farrowing crate. The mat temperature was lowered over the next 15–20 days as the piglets adjusted to their new environment. (Less stress, faster weight gain.)

diplomas. And you know what? The number of dealers entering implements in competition went up instead of down. So the ISAS scuttled the machinery competition altogether. And you know what? The number of dealers bringing implements to the Fair for display and sale went up even further.

So what were those dealers showing off? Plows, harrows, corn planters, reapers, threshing machines, fanning mills and corn crushers, but no combines retailing for $200,000! No stock trailers, farrowing crates, lawn mowers, grain storage bins and handling facilities. Today, such products are scattered throughout 20 acres in the southwest corner of the grounds. It's here that Don Van Houweling, owner of Van Wall Group in Perry, spends 11 days every August. You can find him and five fellow John Deere dealers under the dome tent, chatting with folks from mid-morning until after supper.

They see the same farmers year after year—brand-loyal people who show up to see what's new and different. And in this age of technology, something always is. For example, back in the '80s, you pushed down on a throttle to make things move. Today, you push a button to send an electrical impulse somewhere to tell something to do something.

"It is complicated," says Mr. Van Houweling, "just like everything else."

Farmers come mostly to look; they'll buy when they get back home. Still, looking is profitable, which is why companies like Franklin Industries, Inc., of Monticello have been setting up shop at the Fair since shortly after the company was founded in 1919. For 46 years, Franklin Industries displayed mostly dairy and barn equipment in the Varied Industries Building, then moved outside the building and added a complete line of waterers, gates and bale feeders—not to mention ornamental fencing, trellises, garden arches and the like. What? You say trellises and arches don't sound like something a farmer needs? Probably not, but it might interest the spouse or just as likely, the city folk.

After all, they look at the farm implement displays too. It's true that most city fairgoers don't have a clue about skid loaders, but they get pretty excited about a John Deere 9400 (weight: 18 tons; cost: $160,000), touching the mighty green monster, walking around it, kicking the tires, climbing aboard and checking out the cab. Then they put the 9400 in perspective: You can buy yourself a tractor or buy yourself a house. (continued on page 182)

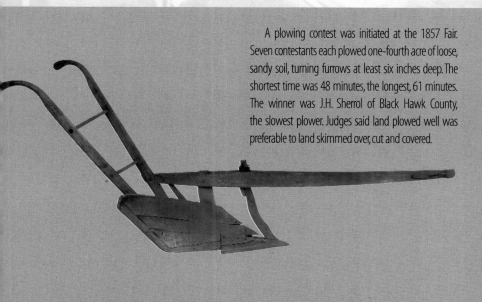

A plowing contest was initiated at the 1857 Fair. Seven contestants each plowed one-fourth acre of loose, sandy soil, turning furrows at least six inches deep. The shortest time was 48 minutes, the longest, 61 minutes. The winner was J.H. Sherrol of Black Hawk County, the slowest plower. Judges said land plowed well was preferable to land skimmed over, cut and covered.

THOSE BEAUTIES

Horses always have been part of the Iowa State Fair, although they didn't officially prance in front of judges until the fourth Fair in 1858. Even so, those beautiful animals have forever enthralled fairgoers. Today, thousands of us wander through the Horse Barn just to look. We say, "No wonder those one-ton draft horses were used to break up the prairie sod." We remark that "the Hackney is poetry in motion."

The breeds are all here—Quarter Horses and American Saddlebred, Appaloosas and Roadster Ponies, Morgans and Arabians. More than 1,600 horses come to compete each August.

Horse and rider go through the motions in a plethora of divisions—country pleasure riding and driving, hunter, fine harness driving and five-gaited events. But the crowd favorites are those six-horse hitches, with the animals

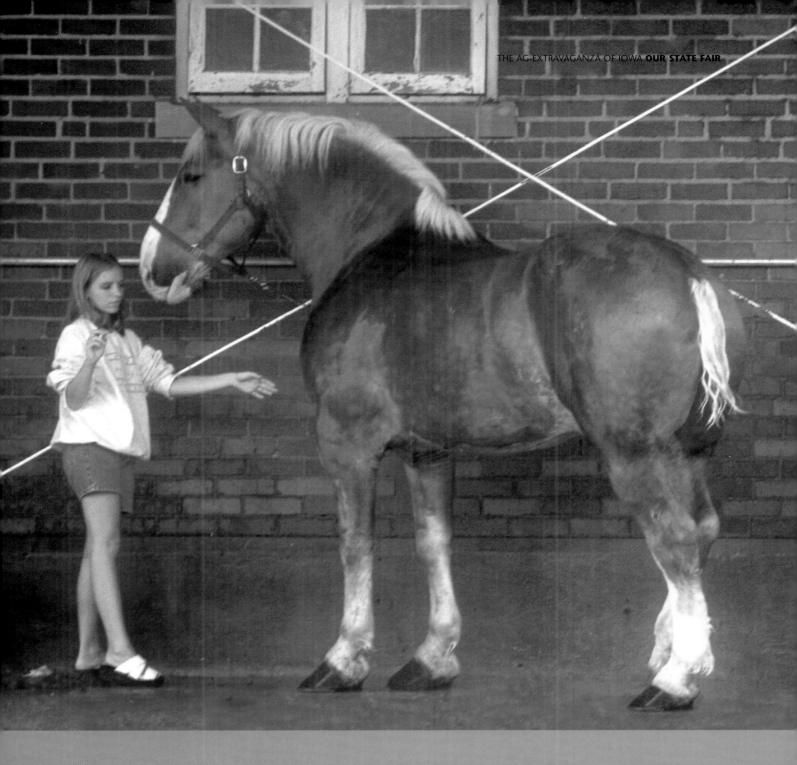

judged by how well they pull the wagon and whether or not they're working together.

Some horse watchers know as much as the riders. Others rarely see a horse, so ask lots of questions. And if they're lucky, they get to give one a pat before they move on to the rest of the Fair!

CENTURY FARMS PROGRAM

After Mary Neu, originally from Germany, and her husband Charles, originally from Luxembourg, migrated to the United States, Mrs. Neu purchased 160 acres south of Arcadia for $28 an acre. The year was 1892.

She died in 1914, and her daughter, Carrie Neu Quinlen, inherited the land. When Mrs. Quinlen died in 1966, nephews Charles and Art Neu inherited the land. By then, it was worth $425 an acre.

Today, the Neu farm—now worth $2,500 an acre—has been recognized by the Iowa Farm Bureau and the Iowa Department of Agriculture as a Century Farm. The designation, awarded to qualified applicants during each State Fair since 1976, recognizes the beauty of such longevity. Art Neu and his wife Mary decided to apply for Century Farm status in 1995 because, "I thought it would be nice," he says. "I knew the farm had been in our family a long, long time." An attorney in Carroll, Mr. Neu remembers helping his Aunt Carrie draft a will when he was "fresh out of law school, and every time she talked about the farm, she cried."

The program pays respect to both the land and its people, who "have contributed greatly to the growth and stability of Iowa agriculture and have provided the management and stewardship to enable this rich prairie soil to bring forth the abundant yields of highest quality food products..." It honors not only production but a way of life.

Between 1976 and 1999, a whopping 2,939 farmers received Century Farm status, which includes a certificate and one of those wonderful metal markers you see out by the road as you drive through rural Iowa.

OH, THOSE KIDS!
FFA

When the Iowa Association of Future Farmers of America joined the national organization in 1929, nobody could have predicted that Traci Henningsen (a girl!) would, one day, show the Grand Champion FFA Market Hog. Or that Ryan Schreck would, one day, build a John Deere Model B tractor so super that strangers who saw it at the Fair wanted to buy it.

My, how things change! The Future Farmers of America—created for farm boys—is now the FFA, comprised of young men and women of all ethnicities from throughout the United States, plus three territories. Thirty-four percent live in urban areas. The FFA's purpose is to help young people develop leadership potential, personal growth and careers through agricultural education.

Every year, more than 900 Iowa FFA members enter livestock and non-livestock competition. Additionally, 200-plus distribute programs and usher at the Grandstand, become stagehands at the free stages or work in the Avenue of Breeds. Some begin work before the Fair starts, helping folks get settled in the Campgrounds.

But back to Ms. Henningsen of DeWitt. In 1999, she took three performance steers, five market lambs, two commercial ewe lambs and eight market hogs to the Fair, including a particular crossbred market barrow. She'd been raising livestock for 10 years, but never a grand champion. Judgment day 1999 for the barrow began at 7:30 A.M. and lasted until 6 P.M.! During the initial judging, the judge looked over about 30 hogs at a time, then penned the top 11 or 12 for the next round. One was Ms. Henningsen's.

"That was exciting," she says.

During the next competition, the judge took a closer look at the penned hogs, then decided Ms. Henningsen's was the best in its class. Her hog went back to the pen to await the next round.

"That was exciting, too," she says.

During the third time in the ring, the judge looked over the best hogs in each of the four classes of heavyweight market barrows and decided Ms. Henningsen's was the division champion. The hog went back to a pen to await the final round.

"I thought, 'Oh, my God, I can't believe this!'" she says.

During the final judging selection, the judge looked at all the division champions in all the weight classes. He talked about criteria for being the Grand Champion Over-All Market Hog. He shared his thought process. Then he hemmed. And hawed. And finally, he announced, "The one that sticks out the most is over in corner—"

"Well, I almost cried," Ms. Henningsen says. "It's a major honor to have the grand champion. Knowing you raised something like that gives you a wonderful feeling."

Ryan Schreck knows that "wonderful feeling," although his didn't come in the show ring. He's the entrepreneur who used his ag mechanics and welding classes at the Carroll Area Agricultural Education Department to produce a model of a half-scale John Deere B tractor. The axle is from an old garden tractor, the back wheels are off a manure spreader, the clutch handle is off a John Deere Model 70, the foot brake is from an H John Deere; he's not sure where the front wheels came from. The project took 300 hours and cost $825.

"The FFA kids we select to work at the Grandstand, with the free stages or in the Campgrounds are the best of the best. You never have a discipline problem with them, and isn't that nice to hear?!"
Jason Brockshus, former ag education instructor and FFA advisor at Sibley-Ocheyedan High School

THE FARM BUREAU
Forever Part of the Fair

When some people think "State Fair," they think "Farm Bureau" too. No wonder! Ever since the Iowa Farm Bureau came to be in 1918, it has been part of the Fair. From the beginning, County Farm Bureaus set up booths and worked with extension services, presenting programs aimed at helping farm families improve their quality of life. In the 1920s, so many bureau members were flocking to the exposition that the Fair Board designated one day each year as Farm Bureau Day. Periodically, a section of the Campgrounds was reserved for Farm Bureau family campers.

For a long time, the state organization maintained a booth in the Varied Industries Building, often using baby chicks to attract attention. (The idea sounded good until it came time to feed the chicks and take care of them at night.) The organization distributed information about everything from how to be a better farmer to why you should vote. (A voting machine was brought in since many people in rural areas had never seen one.) The booth kept expanding until it was 68 feet long. Then in 1981, the bureau moved outside, establishing Farm Bureau Park on the Grand Concourse, east of Varied Industries. There, you can relax on the grass or take up space on a bench and guzzle cold water. Meanwhile, thanks to mazes, posters and puppeteers, your kids can learn about how food grows and why soybeans are good for you.

Since 1992, the Farm Bureau has sponsored the Ag Challenge for farmers under 35. Just like the old college bowl competition, teams compete at the county level. To make it to the big time, you have to know a lot of stuff, such as: How many eggs per year does the average hen lay? (217) and What does the dark color of the soil indicate? (presence of organic matter)

The bureau also challenges folks' grill skills in the Outdoor Cookout Contest. Originally called the Cookout King Contest, the event began in 1964, in response to consumer concerns that eating meat wasn't healthy. These days, County Farm Bureaus, with support from commodity organizations, send their best men, women and teens to Des Moines, where they set up grills on the Grand Concourse, then baste and sear their way to fame while filling the air with the aromas of pork, beef, turkey, lamb and poultry. There's even a showmanship division for people who set a clever table.

Best of all—if you hang around the grills long enough, you may get a free sample!

"I'd just made it for show and parades, but my advisor told me I should bring it to the (1999) Fair," said Mr. Schreck. He brought back first-place gold in the large exhibits competition and received several offers to buy the model. "I knew somebody would probably offer, and that's nice," he says. "But I made something special and I could never sell it." (continued on page 188)

The service component of FFA causes members of the North Polk Community High School Chapter to get up at 5 A.M. every day during the Fair to take care of the Avenue of Breeds. Located in the southwest corner of the Swine Barn, the Avenue has been around since the early '70s. It houses 60 to 70 breeds of cattle, swine, sheep, horses, chickens, rabbits, ducks, geese and turkeys, not to mention ostrich, elk, emus and llamas (appropriately classified as exotics) and game fish (in tanks in pens). They're on display throughout the Fair, which offers marvelous one-stop shopping for farmers, free advertising for breeders and an up-close-and-personal look for everybody! FFA members are on hand to talk with fairgoers about the breeds.

185

THE PARADE OF CHAMPIONS

The only thing better than a parade is several parades, each chock-full of 4-H and FFA winners. Every year, both organizations salute the best of their best as members parade the champions and reserve champions in livestock competition. Families, friends and a sea of supporters fill the Livestock Pavilion to watch the kids and their animals parade around the ring. Also recognized are winners in other animal divisions as well as in non-livestock exhibits. It is truly a feel-good time!

4-H

When 4-H-er Jessica Hanna of LaPorte City and Bell, her Pony of America, trot out of the Show Ring every year at the State Fair, they've earned themselves ribbons—including purple ones. That's nice, but what's more important in that great scheme of things is that Ms. Hanna's knowledge of and love for horses—fostered in part by 10 years' worth of 4-H experiences—helped her decide to pursue a career teaching about the care and training of horses.

Ms. Hanna shows what 4-H is about: learning and doing. The organization grew out of an interest in helping rural youth, primarily by encouraging public school teachers to establish boys' and girls' clubs. The Smith-Lever Act of 1914 enabled county agents and local leaders to organize 4-H clubs. From the beginning, members worked on projects. In 1999, more than 7,000 young people from country and city alike entered 9,500-plus exhibits in Iowa State Fair competition. Some brought cattle or pigs or food or clothing. (And some probably brought cattle *and* pigs *and* food *and* clothing.) Such categories have been part of 4-H since it first showed up on the fairgrounds in the early '20s. But these days new categories are popping up too—from dairy goats to photography.

Today's 4-H-ers also do things differently than their parents and grandparents. For example, demonstrations used to center around how to do something. Now, young people may show you the how, but they also talk about the why as they share information about an idea or issue. Exhibits, too, used to be evaluated on standard

expectations for that item. "We'd say, 'This is what we expect of a blouse or a loaf of bread,'" says Shirley Stakey, state program specialist for 4-H Youth Development. "Today, we ask the 4-H-er to tell us what was achieved by the exhibit, what was learned in the process and how to use that information." Is it surprising, then, that the 4-H Exhibit Hall buzzes with activity from morning until night?

But, hey! The barns are buzzing, too, as 1,900 4-H-ers each year wash and brush and exercise their animals in anticipation of the big show in the ring. Here, too, just showing up for the show isn't enough. Competitors must demonstrate an understanding of issues, such as rate of weight gain, quality of carcass and quality of meat in the carcass. Through the Premier Exhibitor Program, some can also take a written test (i.e., what ingredient is missing from this feed ration?) and then discuss topics such as the future of the industry the animal's species.

There was one change—in 1996—that didn't work out. Officials decided to award 3,500 non-livestock competitors the same multicolored ribbons to recognize participation, rather than the traditional blue, red and white ribbons that recognize standards of achievement. They noted that the competitors already had been named champions at their county fairs, so the question became: Why re-evaluate an exhibit that's been declared a champion?

Public reaction to the ribbon decision was as if someone ate all the red jellybeans from the jar. Linda Mohning of Remsen introduced a plank in the state's Republican Party platform assailing "the encroachment of socialism" in 4-H. *The Des Moines Register* carried articles about the controversy on its front page, prompting a slew of letters complaining that the change challenged not just a cherished program but a way of life.

The multicolored ribbons were one part of a pilot project; participants liked other aspects of the experiment, such as one-on-one discussions with judges. But the next year, the ribbons were blue, red and white again.

STRUCTURES

"*I was asked to do a feasibility study of the State Fair building complex to determine if the buildings were of such quality that the Iowa State Fair could be listed on the National Register of Historic Places. Once the study was complete, I said yes, definitely, the Fair should be listed. The complex contains a representative collection of almost all architectural styles for most of the past 200 years...[plus] each of the architects involved respected the designs of those preceding architects.*"

Bill Wagner
FAIA Preservation Architect

197

Sometime, you really ought to walk around the fairgrounds when there's nothing going on out there. No State Fair. No livestock shows. No arts and crafts festivals. Nothing.

And then what?

And then, you can take time to notice the buildings—how unique each one is and how beautifully they all blend together. It was no accident that this happened, but rather careful planning for more than a century. While you're ambling around on the grounds, think, too, about the Iowa State Fair Blue Ribbon Foundation. Without it, our fairgrounds could, by now, look much different.

Here's why. Most State Fair buildings were constructed before 1920. Because they were unheated, Iowa's freeze-thaw winters had taken their toll. By the late 1970s, loose mortar, sagging roofs, rotting

windows and unsafe wiring were robbing the fairgrounds of its dignity. Although the Fair was operating in the black, neither profits nor legislative appropriations were enough to curtail the crumbling. Despite the fairgrounds' listing on the National Register of Historic Places, the prospect of a gradual shutdown of unsafe facilities loomed. Finally, in 1991, the Legislature authorized creation of a foundation to raise restoration funds. The Iowa State Fair Blue Ribbon Foundation came into being two years later. The foundation's charge is to conduct a major capital campaign for renovation and preservation of the fairgrounds—with a vision for the future. The Fair Board appointed Gladbrook farmer John Putney as the first executive director. He was no stranger to the Fair, having been a long-time cattle exhibitor, president of the Sale of

Champions and beef superintendent. Mr. Putney brought with him Beth Reinig-Greiner, a Harlan native and former staff person for U.S. Senator Charles Grassley.

Today, Mr. Putney, a full-time staff and college interns work year-round, pursuing capital fundraising, government relations and annual sponsorship procurement. They have raised millions of dollars from individuals, corporations, legislative appropriations, in-kind services and grants. The first campaign was based on a contingency pledge by Pioneer Hi-Bred International, Inc. Exceeding the challenge in two years, the foundation moved into its second campaign. In 1997, Des Moines developer William Knapp provided a "challenge gift" of $1 million for renovations of the Varied Industries Building. To date, it is the largest private donation.

The foundation also educates the public, corporations and the Legislature about the Fair's rich history and how monetary donations will preserve that history. Such education has spurred Iowans to buy bricks, trees, benches, T-shirts, mugs, bottled water and more. They donate money through the Corn Dog Checkoff on their individual Iowa tax return forms. They munch corn dogs at the annual Corn Dog Kickoff while they bid at the auction. And they belong to clubs and organizations that sponsor events to benefit the foundation. That sends a message to legislators about the significance the Fair holds for their constituents and the necessity for the State to support renovation and preservation efforts.

The foundation's goal is to raise $60 million by the Fair's sesquicentennial year of 2004. After that, the foundation will keep serving its supporters and programs, as well as be available for future giving and estate planning.

Lucky, that Blue Ribbon Foundation. It has inherited a treasure—albeit one that requires some serious fixing. Already, the foundation's efforts—from restoration of buildings and the Campgrounds to the creation of the Pella Plaza and Hy-Vee Fun Forest—are noticed and appreciated by all of us as we join hundreds of thousands who fill up the fairgrounds each August—and by each of us as we go about our own lives.

Perhaps, in the end, there's a bit of Robert McFarlin Sr. in anyone who loves the Fair and the fairgrounds. In the quiet of spring evenings, this man drives to the fairgrounds from his eastside home. He sits down in front of the Administration Building, takes off his shoes and puts on his roller skates. He sets his headphones to "good, soft music." Then he glides alone through the fairgrounds—by the Grandstand and past the Varied Industries Building to the Main Gate, back up by the Cattle Barn and over to Ye Old Mill.

In 1934, Mr. McFarlin's father brought him here for the first time, to see an auto race. He was 6 years old, and he's been coming back ever since.

It's usually dark when Mr. McFarlin finally takes off his skates. By then, the buildings are bathed in streetlight, but he says you can still see their beauty.

And now, because of the Blue Ribbon Foundation, so will his grandchildren and beyond.

BUTTERFLY GARDEN

ESTABLISHED 1986
BY THE IOWA NONGAME PROGRAM
DEPARTMENT OF NATURAL RESOURCES
IN COOPERATION WITH
THE IOWA STATE FAIRGROUNDS

PIONEER HALL—KING OF THE HILL

Pioneer Hall reigns atop a big hill. Such a location ensures that everyone who comes to the Fair can view the magnificent wooden structure with its high ceiling and distinctive cupola.

Still, it is amazing that Pioneer Hall stands atop that hill, considering it was built for the 1886 Fair—the first Fair at the permanent location. Of the 67 buildings constructed for that event, only Pioneer Hall remains.

Typical of exposition halls of the era, it's been everything by now—a poultry building, an employees' dormitory and a storage facility. Today, the hall houses the Museum of Iowa Agriculture, as well as some bats, who roost high up in the wooden rafters by day and swoop through the vast openness of the hall in the silence of Iowa nights. An old but endangered species, they seem to know when the hall belongs to fairgoers and when it belongs to them.

In Pioneer Hall, Iowans connect with their heritage. The Sunday before the Fair starts, people bring in their antique entries for judging and display. Throughout the Fair, the old hall vibrates with activity: Fiddlers fiddle; potters throw clay; basket makers weave reeds. Watch the blacksmith and furniture maker ply their trades. Or drop by the 1920s print shop to hunt-and-peck your name on a Line-O-Type machine. Gather with the regulars for breakfast, lunch and dinner—and stop back in between for a glass of really zippy lemonade.

It's here that you hear dulcimer music or clap for the cloggers. It's here that wives call husbands, kids call moms and men grow beards. Years ago, women used to throw rolling pins, but officials worried that an airborne pin might soar out of control. (Not intentionally, but some contestants have hit cars.) So today, the rolling pin stays in the kitchen, and the ladies throw rubber chickens filled with sand. "Women waiting in line to throw that rubber chicken say, 'You know, I didn't really mean to come to the Fair and do this,'" says Regina Pirtle, Pioneer Hall superintendent. "But now they are going to throw that rubber chicken, and we know the Fair will never be the same for them again. Looking at things, drinking lemonade, eating a corn dog and going home is one thing; participating is another. Pioneer Hall is like going to Grandma's and discovering that she still has a front porch swing."

Life in Pioneer Hall is slower and without all the commercials. It's yesterday's Fair, when the hustle and bustle were relegated to space outside the fence. It's people who come together for no particular reason other than to have fun.

Pioneer Hall wears well the dignity of those Fairs long past. It has earned that place of honor on the top of the hill.

OH, THE VARIETY
IN THE VARIED
INDUSTRIES BUILDING

Two years after completion of the Grandstand, the Machinery Hall/Varied Industries Building brought under one roof a myriad of commercial displays. With its low walls and red brick corner piers, the building today houses 2 1/2 acres of exhibit booths, making it one of the largest, open-air exhibition halls in the Midwest. One swing through the building and you can buy big things like windows and water softeners, or little things like belt buckles and turquoise rings. Check out the classes offered at Lamoni's Graceland College or LaJames College of Hairstyling in Des Moines. Sign on to support Pheasants Forever or the John Birch Society. Play an organ or push a button and watch the organ play all by itself. Work on your apple slush while you listen to somebody explain why your life won't be complete until you own a set of encyclopedias. You'll bump into 100 people, who all will say, "Excuse me." You'll forget which aisle you went down last. You'll sign up for a ton of free stuff. Then, come next year, you'll wander through the Varied Industries Building (soon to be renovated into a year-round facility) and do the same thing all over again. Hey, if you didn't, where would you ever get your yardsticks?

THE PELLA PLAZA

South of the Ag Building is a slice of Iowa's great outdoors—the Pella Plaza, where your county's flag is flying. This little gem celebrates the state: Shade is courtesy of Iowa Red Oaks and Serviceberrys; beauty is courtesy of Iowa Purple Coneflowers, Prairie Dropseeds and Little Bluestem (planted in orderly rows, just as corn and soybeans were planted on the prairie); boulders and limestone are courtesy of Iowa quarries. The meandering walk reflects Iowa's slow prairie rivers; the straight walks cut through the curves, just as our gravel roads cut up mile sections.

Benches, shade and about as much quiet as you can find at the Fair invite adults to come sit a spell. Fountains on either end of the plaza invite kids to come stand over the sprays, which cause those youngsters to yelp, splash, romp and leave dripping wet. But hey, a couple of swoops down the Super Slide and they're dry again.

Steel Amphitheatre and Race Track,
Iowa State Fair Grounds,
Des Moines, Iowa.

Before the days of sound systems, a gentleman named Rube Leibman walked from one end of the Grandstand to the other, making announcements with a megaphone.

Steel Amphitheatre, State Fair Grounds, Des Moines, Iowa.
Length 380 feet. Depth 109 feet. Seats 8500 people.

THAT GRAND GRANDSTAND

Oh, if only buildings could talk! What that Grandstand would say—not just about the shows but also about all of the audiences who first began filing through its gates in 1909! The steel, brick and concrete structure has burned white-hot with feats of speed and endurance—from racing horses to buzzing airplanes to auto races. The building—all four acres of it— bathes in the glitter of superstars like Liza Minnelli; it shudders from the stomping and clapping for Reba McEntire; it harbors memories of American classics like Bob Hope and Red Skelton. Originally built to hold 10,000, it was enlarged to seat an additional 5,000 in 1927. At that time, both ends and the back of the building were faced with brick and terra-cotta, giving the appearance of an immense exposition hall rather than an amphitheater. Beneath it all are ground-floor classrooms and small auditoriums that have witnessed more demonstrations than you can imagine! And in front of it is a track that's about as long as three football fields.

THE CULTURAL CENTER

The Cultural Center—that poured-concrete building just a bit south and west of Pioneer Hall—has a past worth writing about!

1. The first structure on the site was the Red Cross Building, a temporary hospital staffed during the Fair by doctors and nurses. Like Pioneer Hall, it was one of the first buildings constructed on the permanent fairgrounds. Unlike Pioneer Hall, the Red Cross Building did not survive.

2. In 1949, the Girls' 4-H Dormitory was constructed on that same site. The dormitory cost $417,000 and was completely paid for out of State Fair earnings. It consisted of three floors of double-decker cots and enough bathrooms to accommodate 500 girls. (Can you even imagine how much giggling went on in that place?!)

3. In 1981, the girls moved to the Boys and Girls Youth Inn, and the photography, fine arts, creative arts and crafts competition took their place. The building then was renamed the Cultural Center.

Actually, it was the *second* building on the fairgrounds to be named the Cultural Center. Several years earlier, officials had changed the name of the Women and Children's Building to the Cultural Center. That building was later demolished. (Sometimes, history gets confusing.)

Today, all's quiet on the Cultural Center's third floor, which remains an unair-conditioned dormitory for demonstrators/exhibitors and staff members. But a lot of stuff is happening everywhere else. On the first floor, people wind their way through the fine arts competition, assessing paintings, sculptures, prints and drawings, pottery, jewelry and fiber projects. They stop awhile to watch demonstrations of metal art or batik or jewelry that comes from polymer clay. They wander into the two-story atrium to see what wild thing somebody's building there this year—wondering how you could top the Legos Capitol? And they literally wait in line to see the photography exhibit. Why

not? They'll either spy somebody they know in one of the photos, or they'll find a photo snapped by somebody they know. (Hey, this is Iowa.)

Much of the second floor has been given over to any creative arts or craft that doesn't require a needle and thread—from traditional china painting and miniature (doll) houses to trendy stamp art. Some competitors and guest artists demonstrate their skills; some may sell their work. Then there's Bill Andrus of Des Moines. He sets up shop on the second floor every August, bringing with him at least one of his stained glass lampshades to enter in competition. Before the Fair is over, Mr. Andrus will donate his lampshade to the Woodcarver's Auction. That's held on the Bill Riley Stage come the last Saturday of the Fair, with wood sculptures and prize-winning meat being auctioned off. Proceeds go to the Blue Ribbon Foundation. "I've gone to the Fair ever since I was a kid," says Mr. Andrus, now 75. "I come to the Fair because I get a lot of joy from

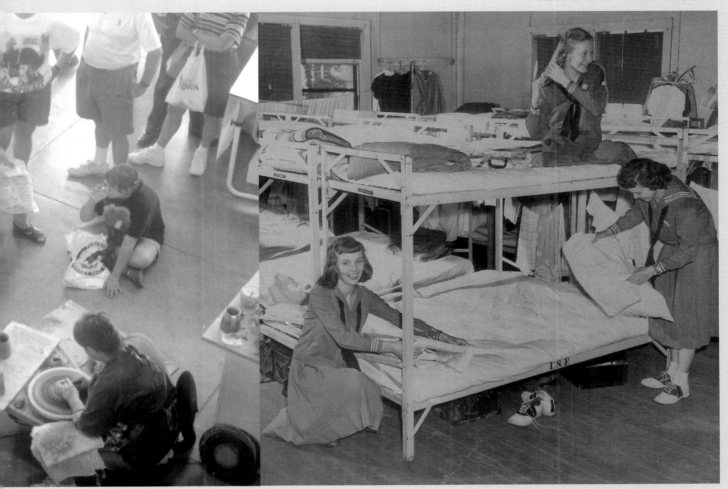

looking at everything and everybody." (Do you suppose he also comes because of the joy he's found in giving back to this blue-ribbon winner of a Fair?)

P.S. Want to know a secret? There's a courtyard behind the Cultural Center, nestled between the building and a lush, green hill. It's quiet back there, relaxing. If you wander there, enjoy a performance by Tubador Gary McCurdy. (He plays the tuba.) And take a look at Dennis R. Lockridge's metal sculpture, Preoccupations. An Iowa Sesquicentennial project, it represents a family visit to the State Fair, with all the good things to do there.

THE ADMINISTRATION BUILDING (AND THE PORCH!)

In 1908, the fairgrounds was graced with the Administration Building. At that time, there was nothing between the main gate at East Thirtieth Street and Grand Avenue and the stately red brick structure trimmed with light-colored stone. Consequently, the Administration Building anchored the west end of the fairgrounds. Today, it houses the year-round State Fair offices as well as providing a residence for Fair Board members during the exposition. But it isn't what goes on inside this magnificent building that fairgoers find so endearing. Rather, it's that porch. Gracefully wrapping itself around the building, the wide veranda beckons kids and adults alike to "come sit a spell." Somehow cool and breezy, even in an Iowa August, the porch serves as a nostalgic reminder of State Fairs past. Plop down and eat your Guinea Grinder or wait while the kids ride the Rock-o-Plane, or simply watch the people walking by as they watch you sitting there. For a whole lot of folks, spending five minutes on that veranda is one of the treats of the Iowa State Fair!

Administration Building, Iowa State Fair Grounds, Des Moines, Iowa.

Bird's Eye View, showing Administration Building and Stock Pavilion, Iowa State Fair Grounds, Des Moines, Iowa.

THE STATE FAIR MUSEUM

If you think the museum looks more like a house, you're right. Probably constructed in the late 1800s as the Polk County Building, it was used by residents of the Polk County Home on Northeast Fourteenth Street in Des Moines on their day-trips to the Fair. The houseguests ate at big tables and rested on second-floor couches and front porch benches.

By the early '70s, few people still lived in the Polk County Home, so the Polk County Building became the Fair's attic—a great place to store stuff. Then, in 1982, it reopened as the official State Fair Museum. And all that stored stuff graduated to displayed treasures for Fair lovers, antique dabblers and the history buffs to ogle over.

Today, the museum is a potpourri of the Fair's past—a fainting couch once used in the Women and Children's Building; an oak rolltop desk used by Fair secretaries until Jim Taylor's tenure; premium books dating from 1879, the Fair's first year in Des Moines; a photograph of Dr. John Clinton, who conducted morning services at Heritage Village's First Church; Baby Mine's performing stand; a landscape map of the proposed permanent Fair site east of Des Moines; and Healthy Baby Contest trophies.

Looking at the picture postcards—which you could buy at just about any drugstore in Iowa, come Fair time—is like going through the family album. And noting the price of the old gate tickets on display reminds you that while life might not have been better back then, it sure was cheaper!

209

Originally, livestock was housed primarily in temporary sheds and pens. But in 1885, the ISAS purchased land for a permanent Fair and, within one year, built 10 horse barns, 10 cattle barns, roofless swine pens and sheep cotes for the 1886 Fair. There were also 50 wells, which supplied enough water for both stock and visitors, plus a level lawn inside the horse track to which "ladies and gentlemen in carriages will be admitted, which is a delightful privilege to that class of people," according to The Iowa State Register.

The frame barns were on the south end of the grounds, close to the railroad lines, which is how animals got to the Fair. The barns were built in circles, with each being equally distant from the show ring in the center. Still, because the structures were hastily built on a tight budget, maintenance became common. Consequently, when the State took over Fair management in 1902, a massive building campaign included new barns that were built in phases, from 1902 until 1936.

THE CATTLE BARN

A brick Cattle Barn—with an office, dining room and sleeping quarters for herdsmen—was completed in 1920. It had stalls for 1,520 head (today, it's up to 2,000). The building was open from one end to the other, making exhibitor locations easily accessible to the public. Plus there were wide aisles and wash racks with hot and cold water for livestock grooming. City water was carried to all parts of the building via an elaborate drainage system that provided perfect sanitation. (At least the 1920 Fair Board reported the sanitation was perfect.)

Today, the barn is used year-round for livestock events, auctions, trade shows and meetings. During a State Fair run, up to 4,000 head will spend a few days there. In special exhibit areas—where dairy and beef cattle are stalled—you can view familiar breeds like Shorthorns and Black Angus, which even city folk recognize! But you can also see exotic and European breeds like Belgian Blue or Gelbvieh—which might fool an Iowa farmer.

The Sale Ring, completed in 1921, was named in 1997 for Don and Orville Penningroth of Wellman after they bequeathed $470,000 from their estate. Don exhibited Shorthorn cattle at the Fair for 60 years; Orville exhibited Poland China Hogs for 25 consecutive years. Both brothers died during the 1990s and are memorialized with a plaque and quotation that reads: "They gave their life's toil to an institution they cherished."

THE LIVESTOCK PAVILION

The Livestock Pavilion is a State Fair staple with its familiar soaring dome, sawdust-covered floor and show-ring atmosphere. Built in 1902 as the first masonry building on the grounds, it features handsome purple brick, arched back openings and stone trim, topped by an enormous three-tiered roof with clerestory glass to bring in daylight. It was ventilated by a fan system that forced in fresh, warm air and drew out foul air at the same time. Today, it is the heart of livestock judging and horse shows.

211

THOSE OTHER BARNS

The Swine Pavilion and Barn and the Horse Barn were begun in 1907; the Sheep Barn, in 1915. Each covers a city block—which is a lot of barn! And, hey, they're pretty! See for yourself next time you're down by the Dean Avenue Gate. Note how the cupolas seem to grow out of the Swine Barn roof. Designed to permit the summer breezes to flow freely, the building features a pattern of 1,100 pens and walkways leading to twin sawdust-covered show rings. Now turn to the Sheep Barn, pausing to admire the art deco terra-cotta carvings of sheep heads decorating the perimeter, as well as the blue and white terra-cotta borders framing its entrances. Then, of course, there's the Horse Barn, all dressed up in different shades of red brick. The interior's subdued and darkish atmosphere blends with the unmistakable odor of hay and horse "apples." Over the years, the barn has housed

some beauties—from thousand-pound draft horses to the miniature steeds.

Do You Know That...

...the ordinary-looking little barn east of the Livestock Pavilion made history in the early 20th century when it was on a Warren County farm owned by the Gammon family of Des Moines. It was in this barn that Warren and Bert Gammon selected animals that had naturally hornless characteristics and, eventually, created a breed of hornless beef cattle, the Polled Hereford. One of only a few breeds to originate in this country, the Polled Hereford earned the Gammons national recognition, including induction into the Polled Hereford Hall of Fame in Kansas City, Missouri. In 1991, the Gammon Barn was moved, pole by pole, to the State Fairgrounds.

...along about 6 o'clock each evening, exhibitors parade almost 1,700 cattle from the Cattle Barn to Hawkeye Breeders Hill two blocks or so to the southeast. There, the cattle are tied up at panels for a night of open-air freshness—no doubt a welcome change after a long day in the barn. Come morning, the animals go back to freshened stalls until it's time to be rinsed off and spiffed up for the show.

...as you walk through the barns, spiders may suddenly dangle before your eyes. (We mean *right* before your eyes.) They could be plastic spiders, perhaps tied onto strings that have been looped over the rafters. And at the other end of those strings may be young male or female exhibitors who happen to be bored. They would appreciate it if you could at least act frightened.

BEYOND THE CATTLE BARN

The Dairy Parlor is just north of the Cattle Barn. In 1968, a picture window was installed so fairgoers could view a "modern" milking operation at work. While it's no longer reflective of today's big-time operations, it's still typical of small dairy farms. Next to the Dairy Parlor is the Midwest Dairy Association Dairy Barn. On a hot, sticky afternoon, sidle up and order a cone or milkshake. While you're slurping away, pause to appreciate all those hardworking cows! Finally, what is now Stockman's Inn on the south side of the barn once was the Beef Palace, a refrigerated area used to display prizewinning beef carcasses. Fairgoers could tell how correct the judges had been in choosing the winners.

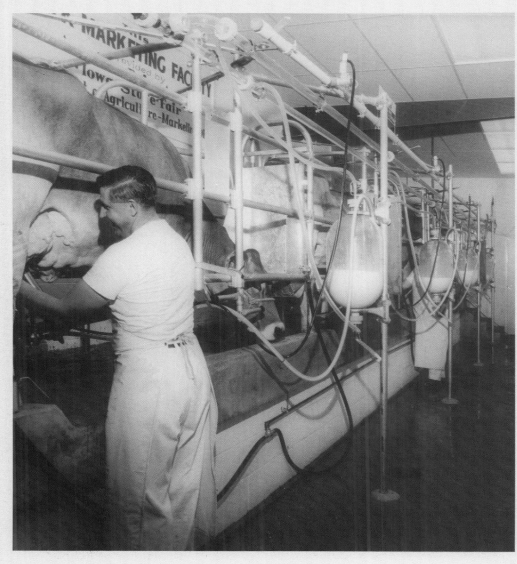

4-H BUILDINGS
AT THE FAIR

Initially, 4-H exhibits were in the Exposition Building, which was constructed for the first permanent Fair in 1886. In 1949, exhibits moved from there into the Education Building under the Grandstand. Then in 1965, they moved on to the Poultry Industries Building, which was renamed the 4-H Exhibits Building. This, incidentally, is the only building President Gerald R. Ford toured during his 1975 visit to the Fair.

The 4-H and FFA boys moved into Hillcrest Dormitory when it was built in 1930 and still use that dorm for overflow. (Bunks aside, plenty of the boys stayed in the barns with their livestock.) In 1940, a majority of the boys moved to the new Youth Inn; in 1981, structural changes turned the building into two dormitories—one half for the boys and the other half for the girls.

Originally, the girls stayed in Flower Hall (later called Pinecrest Lodge), another of the structures built for the first Fair. That was torn down in 1949, and the girls moved into a new Girls' 4-H Dormitory where they stayed until 1981. That year, the dormitory became the Cultural Center, and the girls moved into their half of the Youth Inn.

YE OLD MILL

Art King of Des Moines spent the 1947 Fair at the Christ Evangelical United Brethren Church stand, which was immediately east of Ye Old Mill. He and others opened the place each morning, did pretty much everything during the day, then closed it up at night. One day, Bonnie Bean and other volunteers from the Staves Memorial Evangelical United Brethren Church Christian Endeavor Youth Group showed up to work. Miss Bean had had several dates with Mr. King, but the relationship wasn't really going anywhere.

Then, Mr. King invited Miss Bean on a boat ride through Ye Old Mill, and during their glide, he gave her a kiss. Eighteen months later, they were married, and in 1999, they celebrated their golden wedding anniversary.

Obviously, Ye Old Mill works!

Built in 1921 (and billed then as Ye Olde Mill), it offered folks a 1,500-foot-long canal ride—which was kind of exciting for dating couples back when things like that were exciting. For a few years in the '60s, Ye Old Mill offered another form of excitement on the last day of the Fair, thanks to Tom and Ted Deets, whose father was maintenance superintendent at the time. They would sneak inside Ye Old Mill, dump detergent into the water and be long-gone before the paddlewheel churned up foam, filling boats with soapsuds (which probably discouraged further kissing).

Eventually, somebody invented a product to prevent foaming, plus the Deets boys grew up. What a shame on both counts!

By the early '90s, Ye Old Mill was high on the repair list. The 8- by 8-inch timbers holding up the open-air building were so full of dry rot and termite damage that you could pick a timber up with one hand. Repair plans changed to replacement plans after a hefty wind brought the mill to the ground in 1996. Happily, a new Ye Old Mill was waiting for fairgoers that August.

THE NATURAL RESOURCES BUILDING

If William Albert were around today, you could thank him for an up-close-and-personal look at some of Iowa's native trout, catfish and northern pike during their annual State Fair appearance in the Natural Resources Building. As state fish and game warden, Mr. Albert pushed for construction of the now-familiar red brick building with its Italian Renaissance detail. (Don't miss the intricately molded swans and eagles on the corners of the roof and frogs around the aquaria.) Still, when construction started in 1919, his dream of an educational facility looked quite different from today.

The original exhibit was a roughly fenced-in tract containing different species of waterfowl and a steel stock tank of native fish. During the next 10 years, walls went up around the aquarium, followed by a roof and, finally, outer walls. Today, thousands tour the aquarium and check out the trumpeter swans, mallard ducks and Canada geese on the pond west of the building.

Until 1981, live wild animals were also on display, brought in from the Wildlife Exhibit at the Ledges State Park. But the exhibit's closing cut off the animal source. (Timing on that closing may not have been better, since public concern over caged animals was growing by the early '80s.)

So nowadays, fairgoers watch birds and ogle fish. And if you stand still long enough, some of the fish may ogle you back. They swim in city water that's been aerated, cooled and treated to retard fish disease. Most fish last the entire Fair, then return "home" to ponds near Rathbun Reservoir until the following year, when they are seined up again and brought to the Fair the day before it opens.

The record holder for State Fair appearances may be Oscar, a rock sturgeon said to weigh 100 pounds plus. He ogled and was ogled for 28 years back in the '50s, '60s and '70s.

MEET YOU AT THE FAIR

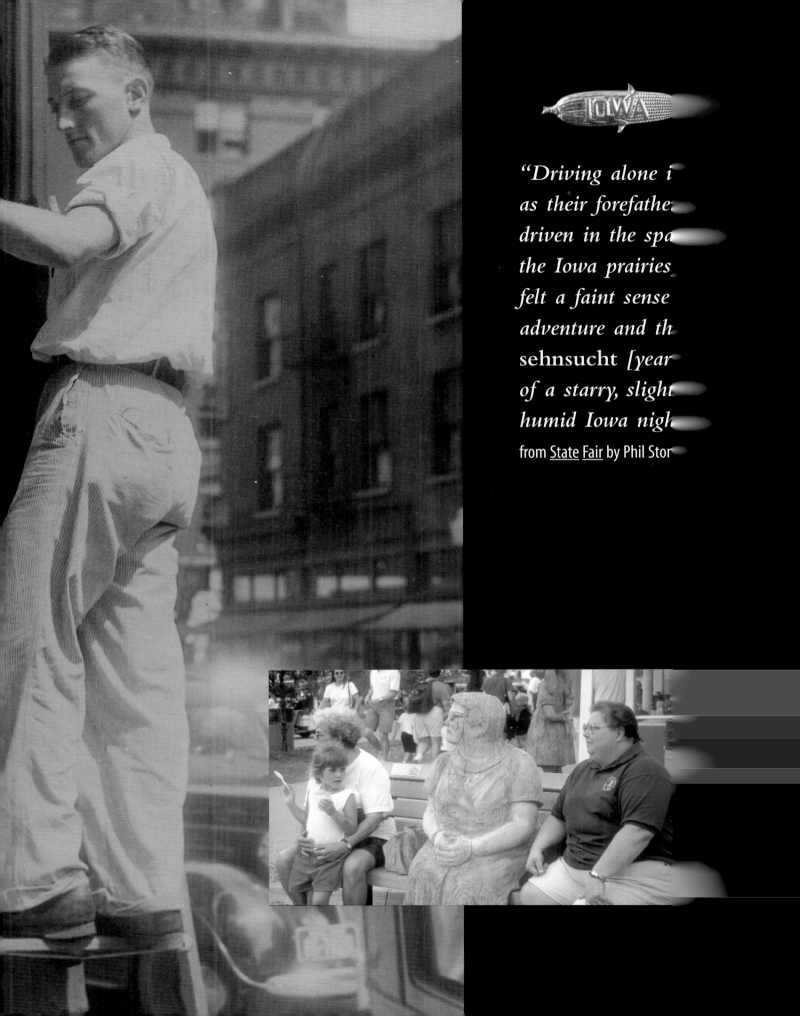

"Driving alone i
as their forefathe
driven in the spa
the Iowa prairies
felt a faint sense
adventure and th
sehnsucht [year
of a starry, slight
humid Iowa nigh
from <u>State</u> <u>Fair</u> by Phil Stor

So, here we are—thousands and thousands of fairgoers, actually millions and millions of fairgoers, when you consider all those who were part of the Iowa State Fair experience long before any of us was a twinkle in somebody's eye. And the beautiful thing about all of us—past, present and even to come—is that we're as diverse as the Fair itself. Some of us spend a day a decade at the Fair; others spend 11 days every summer. Some of us live in extravagant houses; others rent efficiency apartments. Some of us live on farms; others have never set foot on a farm. Some of us can't snap enough photos of our youngsters as they race from one kiddie ride to the next; others are glad the kids are grown so we can sit quietly and watch fancy horses prance around in a ring. Some of us know every breed of cattle in the barn; others wouldn't go near the barn without a nose plug. Some of us sip lemonade; others chug beer.

Some of us camp at the Fair; others don't. The thing is, those campers might be having more fun.

221

TENT CITY

A Story All Its Own

Camping at the Fair is not new. In 1854, folks traveled to the first Fair in Fairfield on foot, horseback, in covered wagons or two-wheeled carts pulled by ponderous oxen. Even before opening day, strangers started drifting into Fairfield, first by scores, then by hundreds and, during the exposition, by thousands. Attendance ran about 7,000 per day. Considering Fairfield's population (1,013) and the fact that it had only three hotels—the Clay, the National and the Restoration House—securing accommodations was tough. Camping was one option. Within two years, attendance was 10,000 per day, which caused Iowa State Agricultural Society (ISAS) Secretary J.H. Wallace to suggest, "Every man bring his blanket or buffalo robe, and then in case he can do no better, he has a bed of his own." After the 1858 Fair in Oskaloosa, Mr. Wallace noted that "a considerable number of the very best ladies in the State were not inside of a house from the time they left home till they returned."

When the Fair finally settled into its permanent Des Moines home in 1886, a hill in the northeast section was designated as the official camping area. Hickory, oak and walnut trees provided welcome shade; columbine, Dutchman's-breeches, Cowslip, Jack-in-the-Pulpit, Sweet William and, of course, dandelions offered refreshing beauty. Plus, the area was just far enough beyond the busy, dusty heart of the Fair that it quickly became home for 2,000. Within two years, the ISAS was stringing electric lights throughout Tent City.

Shortly after the turn of the century, so many fairgoers were tenting that *Wallaces Farmer* suggested the Campgrounds be platted,

SAFE AND SOUND

Those in charge of the 1863 Fair in Dubuque chose a "good, healthy" location for the Campgrounds, then paid a guard to look after things and preserve order day and night.

Things sure have changed since that one-man safety force. For a long time, the State Fair tapped civilian friends to police the grounds. In 1889, "several pickpockets and sneak thieves working at the Fair," were handcuffed and taken to town for a speedy trial. In 1914, management arranged with the state militia to furnish two companies of guardsmen—one from Red Oak and the other from Fort Dodge—to work the Fair in their spiffy military uniforms. During the '20s and '30s, farmers riding their own horses served as mounted police, patrolling the fences for potential trespassers.

Today, security during the Fair costs $209,000. That includes payroll for the Iowa State Fair Patrol's five full-time employees, 28 part-timers and the 85–100 others hired specifically for the Fair. It also pays for equipment, supplies and expenses related to the Iowa State Patrol, which is present during the Fair.

And what is the Fair Patrol's biggest challenge during those 11 days in August? People's safety and crowd control at events such as when Robbie Knievel jumps over semi-trailer trucks. Still, horse shows, cattle sales, expos, craft shows and races keep security busy all year long.

streets laid out, numbered and named, plus a record kept of the occupants. At the very least, it was suggested that campers make an effort to erect their tents in an orderly fashion.

By the 1930s, one-quarter of all fairgoers were camping. The luckier ones had prize plots at the top of the hill—lots sometimes staked out by grandparents or great-grandparents almost a half century earlier. State Fair author Phil Stong wrote about that in another of his books, Strangers Return, recalling that his "was a good tent site that

grandfather staked out in 1892, near the top of the hill where the breeze could reach it under fine shade trees…"

Kenneth Fudge of Creston was camping with his family before Mr. Stong was ever published. His first trip was in 1924, when he was 6 months old. The family rented a tent from Des Moines Tent and Awning Company, pitched it on a cement slab and stayed three days. Mother Eva fixed the meals (and baked bread) on a three-burner kerosene stove with an oven that they'd brought along on the back of their Whippet. Mr. Fudge remembers summers so hot "you could break eggs on University Avenue and the white would set." He also remembers Fairs so cheap that "my friend and I would each bring $10 for three days, go to the barns, see all the free stuff, ride a few rides and go home with money leftover."

When Mr. Fudge married Bernice Reed, they came to the Fair, pitched their tent on a bed of straw, and Bernice became the cook. Eventually, the tent gave way to a truck with tarps, then to a fifth wheel and, finally, to an air-conditioned motor home. Plus, the Fudge children have had children and grandchildren, and the

By the 1930s, one-quarter of all fairgoers were camping. The luckier ones had prize plots at the top of the hill—lots sometimes staked out by grandparents or great-grandparents almost a half century earlier.

Bernice and Kenneth Fudge

During the Depression, people would park on University Avenue, then picnic on the grass outside the gates. They had a perfect view of the Grandstand events (especially high-wire acts) and the Midway and could still hear the music.

campsite has been upgraded to the lot at C Avenue and Wallace Circle—which, in case you don't know, is prime real estate. "You can see everybody coming and going," Mr. Fudge explains.

The extended Fudge family attends every Fair, sits on porch chairs under the awning, with a refrigerator within arm's reach, and talks with "neighbors" who have become friends. "Coming here is a tradition," Mrs. Fudge says. "It's the natural thing to do in August."

They still shop at the Campgrounds Grocery, but Mrs. Fudge no longer cooks all the meals. She keeps the refrigerator and the cupboards stocked, but the kids can also go down to the fairgrounds and eat whenever they want. The Fudges have been interviewed by an international television crew and have won the Campgrounds Lighting Contest so many times that they quit entering, "to give somebody else a chance."

Ah, yes—that lighting contest. The idea originated in 1984 when Bill Fisher, the Fair's assistant manager, observed that some trailers were decked out in plastic flowers, leaves, vines and fruit, plus Pepsi bottles that lit up. Certainly, this was creativity in search of a reward. One night, he unscrewed a horse from the top of a horse show trophy and replaced the horse with a yellow bug light. Then, Mr. Fisher, his brother-in-law Marty Gillespie and the State Fair queen wandered through the Campgrounds until they found the most—um—unusually decorated trailer, and gave the owner the first-place trophy in the "new outdoor lighting contest." A week later, a photo and story showed up in *The Jasper County Tribune*. A year later, more trailers sported lights and homespun decorations.

And that, my friends, is how contests sometimes originate. Each year, a dozen campsites participate in the official contest, although

hundreds of others sport lights. Judging is by a committee that rides through the Campgrounds in golf carts, occasionally accepting free drinks and appetizers from contestants.

POWER UP

Campers can thank Ben Crawford every time they flip the lighting contest switch. Actually, everybody can thank Ben Crawford every time any switch is flipped. That's because from 1946 until 1990, he served as chief electrician, converting the fairgrounds' power system from a mass of wooden poles with wire strung in all directions to an underground power system that provides enough energy to run a medium-sized city.

Mr. Crawford and wife Pope raised a large family in their fair-grounds home. Son Ben Jr. is now the Fair's chief electrician. One of his brothers is also an electrician, two others are carpenters and another is an electrical engineer. While sister Grace didn't follow in everybody else's footsteps (she owns a small business), she joins the rest of Pope and Ben's children and grandchildren, who return to the Fair each year either to work or visit their old home.

STATE FAIR—
THE BOOK, THE
MOVIE, THE MUSICAL

Even before Phil Stong immortalized the
Fair in his book State Fair, he was connected to
the event. His grandfather, George Duffield of
Keosauqua, was on the ISAS Board, and his
niece, Duffy Lyon, is the Butter Cow Lady. Plus,
as a young reporter for *The Des Moines
Register*, Mr. Stong covered the Fair.

Still, he preferred being an author to a
journalist, and eventually settled in New York
to write. Twelve unpublished novels later, his
agent called to say that publishers were
looking for a "Sinclair Lewis story more
humorous and fairer to small town people
than Main Street." And that's how Phil Stong
came to write State Fair in New York City.

State Fair is the story of a 1920s farm
family that goes every year to the Fair. This
particular year, father Abel Frake is focused on
Blue Boy, whom he proudly refers to as "the
finest Hampshire stud boar in the world," an
animal certain to win best-of-show. Mother
Melissa is determined to take home blue

ribbons for her mincemeat and pickles. Childre
Margy and Wayne are more into romance. Marg
bumps into Pat Gilbert, a *Register* reporter, and the
fall in love; Wayne falls for a Fair singer name
Emily. All seems wonderful till it's time to retur
home. So, Pat and Margy and Wayne and Emily sa
good-bye—interesting considering the readin
audience's aversion to unhappy endings.

When the book was published in 1932,
became an immediate success. Hollywood release
a film the next year starring Will Rogers an
Janet Gaynor. The next decade, Rodgers an
Hammerstein remade State Fair into a musica
movie starring Dick Haynes and Jeanne Crain. Th
score included "It's a Grand Night for Singing!" an
"It Might as Well Be Spring," which garnered a

Blue Boy's acting career was cut short a year
after State Fair came out when he died. His
obituary in the February 6, 1934, issue of Time
magazine read—Died: Blue Boy, prize hog, film
actor, star of the Phil Stong-Will Rogers cinema
State Fair; of overeating and overgrooming; in
Hollywood.

Academy Award. Yet another movie musical, released in 1962, starred Pat Boone and Ann-Margret, but the setting was the Texas State Fair, for goodness sake! In 1995, an adaptation of the 1945 musical premiered in Des Moines, starring John Davidson and Kathryn Crosby. Codirected by James Hammerstein, son of Oscar, it went to Broadway but closed after 118 performances.

We return now to the novel, which made Phil Stong a wealthy man. He wrote novels for 25 more years, but none hit it big like State Fair. In March 1957, Mr. Stong was diagnosed with cancer of the mouth. On April 26, he wrote to his brother, claiming the disease had been cured. Later that day, Phil Stong died of a heart attack.

THE WOMEN AND CHILDREN'S BUILDING

People still talk about this place, which went up east of the Agriculture Building in 1914. About how it stood so stately atop the hill, just beyond a horse-shoe driveway outlined by hydrangeas—all red brick, white stone trim and red tile roof—encircled by a magnificent porch that afforded a panoramic view of the grounds. (Did we mention that grapevines were draped over the wrought iron railings?)

And that was just the outside!

Inside were a fireproof art gallery nice enough to attract Grant Wood; a model school-room with cloakrooms, lighting and ventilation; two auditoriums; an entire floor devoted to resting and relaxing; a nursery and sand-floor playroom where children were left with "trained nurses" for a nominal fee.

"What a shame the building's gone," folks say. But that's what happens when rain leaks through a tile roof, and when grading inadvertently redirects the flow of underground water into a building, when grapevines trap damaging moisture against bricks and mortar, and when disrepair graduates to deterioration. And when there is no money to fix such problems.

In the fall of 1980, after contractors salvaged the building's heavy timber and wooden framework, the Women and Children's Building came down, ultimately to be replaced by the Fairview Stage.

MAKE WAY FOR WOMEN

This may come as a surprise: President Theodore Roosevelt had a hand (albeit indirectly) in our fine State Fair. In 1907, he created the Country Life Commission to study rural life, including the life of the farmer's wife. "There is no more important person, measured in influence upon the life of the nation, than the farmer's wife," the President wrote, "[and] no more important home than the farm country home, and it is of national importance to do the best we can for both."

Two years later, the commission suggested—among other things—modernizing the farm home and helping rural women become more efficient at household management. It reasoned that this would help educate rural Iowa women—who were more isolated than town women. The commission's aim was to make farm life easier and, consequently, more attractive. Iowa State College, its Extension Service and 4-H were in the best position to respond to that call for education. And where better for the organizations to reach and teach farm women than at the Iowa State Fair. (continued on page 239)

LITTLE LOST KIDS

"'Please return this child to *Wallaces Farmer* pavilion,' read the tag attached to the dress of a 7-year-old belonging to one of the farmer families. A very sensible precaution and a very easy way to make sure that if the child should be separated from its parents, little time would be lost in finding it. One fine thing about the Iowa Fair is that almost no harm is likely to come to children who may become separated from their parents. They find friends on every hand, and if there is anything about the child to indicate where it belongs, a dozen are ready to volunteer to see that it gets there safely and promptly."

Iowa Department of Agriculture's
1913 Yearbook

237

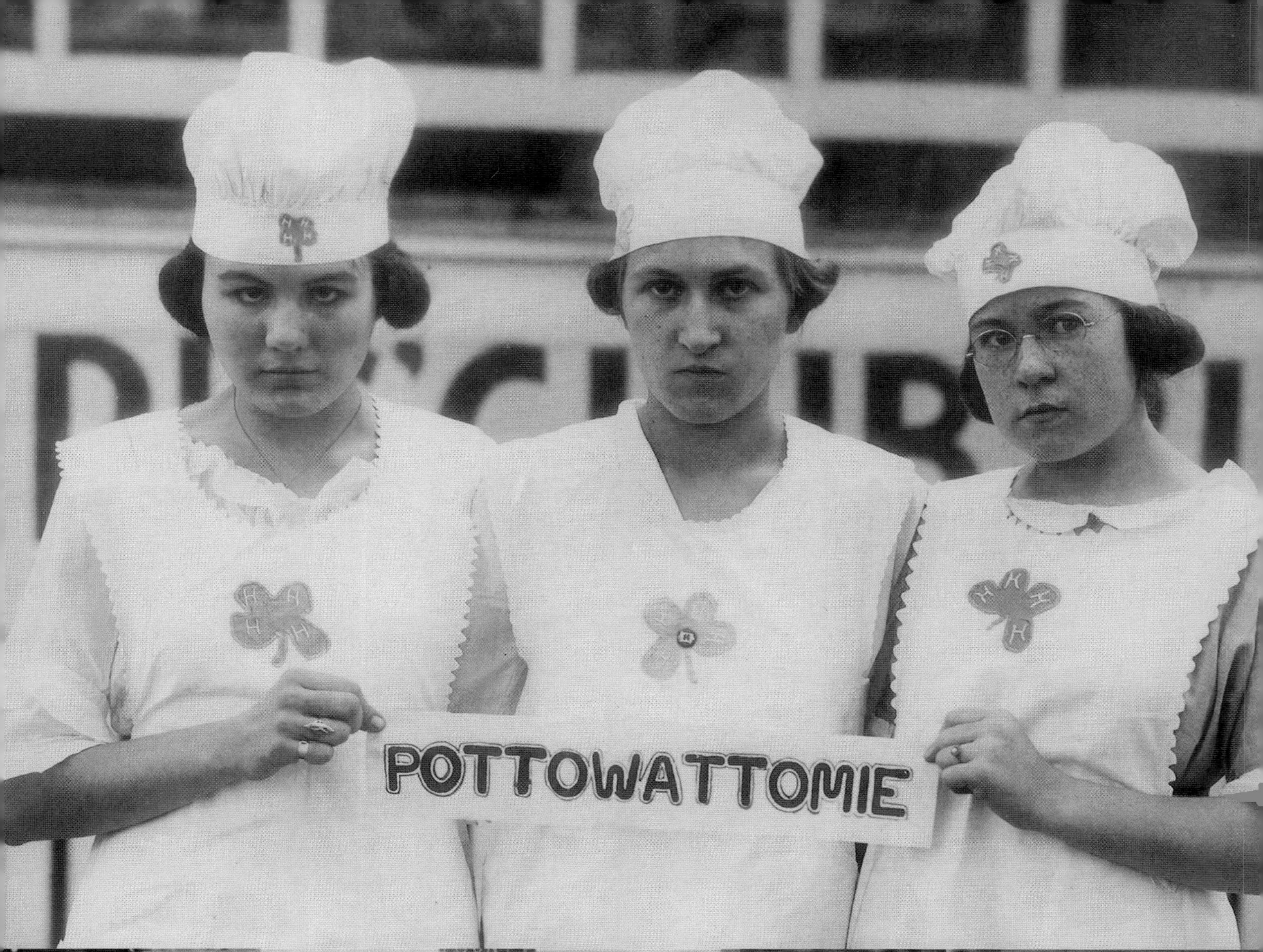
POTTOWATTOMIE

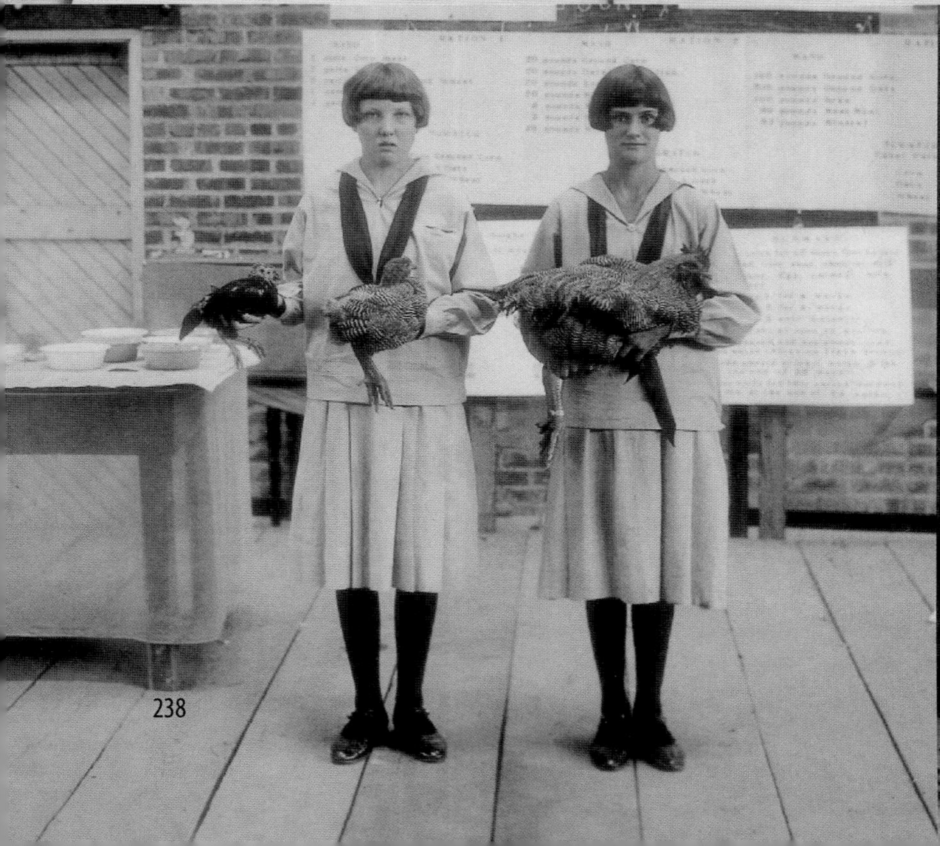

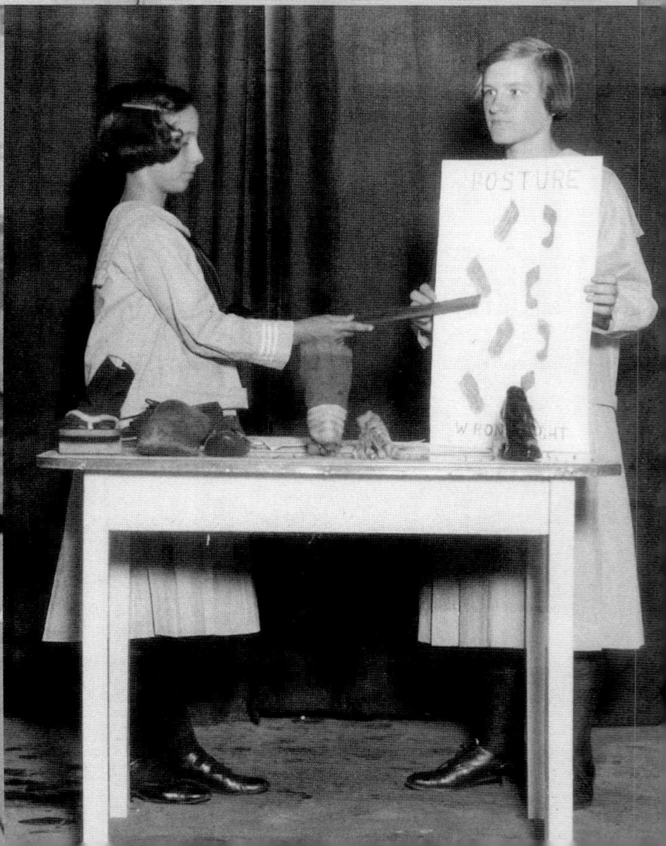
POSTURE

Women always had actively participated at the Fair. When the exposition settled into its permanent home in 1886, the Woman's Suffrage Association and the Woman's Christian Temperance Union were the first organizations to request space for cottages on the fairgrounds. By the turn of the century, fairs included a Woman's Day. And in 1903, Fair Secretary J.C. Simpson turned the Horticultural Hall into the Woman's Rest Building and Emergency Hospital, commonly referred to as the Women's Building. However, Mr. Simpson designated it as a place where women and children could rest, not a place where women's clubs could meet. Consequently, the Iowa Congress of Mothers (later to become the PTA) lobbied the Legislature for money to build a real Women and Children's Building, which opened 11 years later.

It was in this building that home economists began changing women's fare at the Fair. Declared Neale S. Knowles, an Iowa State home economics instructor, "With the Women's Building used to the full extent of its possibilities, the State Fair program becomes a more vital factor in the great national effort to increase interest in 'right living,' in the effort to reduce disease, poverty, crime and all phases of inefficiency, to the minimum."

That was one tall order, tackled mainly through educational exhibits dealing with food and nutrition, clothing, home furnishing, child development and home management. Unlike the familiar exhibits of jams and jellies lined up in a row, these exhibits consisted of maps and charts indicating how people could improve their "household habits." Additionally, because

Unlike the familiar exhibits of jams and jellies lined up in a row, these exhibits consisted of maps and charts indicating how people could improve their "household habits."

The Iowa Homestead *reported that women in one township had used pedometers and "saved 40,000 steps by 'changing their ways.'"*

this endeavor to educate Iowa's farm women was set up on a county-wide basis, extension workers reported on their county's progress. Consider the Western Pottawattamie County Results submitted for the 1928 Fair: ...787 [persons] using more greens; 806 serving tomatoes twice a week; 181 using more economy in buying; 449 serving simpler desserts; 98 improving quality of cottage cheese....

You think that's detailed? The *Iowa Homestead* reported that women in one township had used pedometers and "saved 40,000 steps by 'changing their ways.'"

Turning education over to the experts made going to the Fair a lot like going to college, only cheaper. For instance, a skit, "Let's Go Shopping," taught women that a store may change its policies because of informed customers; a lecture, "Your Money's Worth in Clothing," centered on understanding labels and manufacturers' terms in the ready-to-wear industry. Mrs. Eugene Cutler, 1938 president of the Iowa Federation of Women's Clubs, pointed out, "Yesterday, we found men and women discussing problems in their own little groups. Today, we have those problems taken up by speakers who are authorities on a given subject…Where we used to talk about the style of a dress, we now are told by trained home economics leaders of methods that can be used to judge the fabric itself and how it should be cleaned."

Gradually, the educational efforts expanded to include the whole family. Exhibits in 1961 focused on goal setting; incorporating music, art and literature into family life; a well-planned house;

personal appearance; successful careers; healthful meals in a gracious setting; and parental responsibility.

Today, lines of demarcation between rural and urban women have disappeared, thanks primarily to the media. Now, programs cover the gamut—from tofu classes to breast cancer.

LET'S EAT!

Dennis Rhodes remembers getting up before dawn on hot August mornings in the late '40s, eating bacon and eggs, helping load the car, then climbing in with his family for what seemed an incredibly long ride from Guthrie Center to Des Moines. It was State Fair day, and when the gates opened at 7 A.M., the Rhodeses' Ford was waiting in line. Had to be if you wanted a plum parking spot under a shade tree. After all, shade helped keep that galvanized tub in the trunk—filled with food and ice—cool until noon, when the family trekked back from the fairgrounds

to the car for lunch. Sitting on blankets, they'd dive into Mom's fried chicken, potato salad, baked beans, chocolate cake and iced tea. Plus, there were those little, unsliced loaves of Colonial Bread you picked up someplace on the grounds.

"It would have been fun to go to a food stand," he says, "but there was just so much money to go around."

Mr. Rhodes, now of West Des Moines, says it seemed like everybody in the parking lot was eating fried chicken and potato salad. "It would have been fun to go to a food stand," he says, "but there was just so much money to go around. If you ate what your mom

Wonder Bars 10¢
Ice Cream On A Stick
Dipped In Chocolate
Rolled In Fine Mixed Nuts

Swift's
Ice Cream

WONDER BAR
ICE CREAM ON A STICK
10¢ Dipped in Chocolate!
Rolled in fine Mixed Nuts

WONDER BAR
ICE CREAM ON A STICK
Dipped in Chocolate!
Rolled in fine Mixed Nuts

HATS

brought, you'd have money to buy lemonade, go on two rides and get a souvenir, which always broke before you got home."

Actually, everybody wasn't eating in the parking lot. Thousands were going through the cafeteria line in Carl and Ted's Dining Hall in the basement of the Administration Building. Opened in 1946 by Carl Cardamon and Ted Sammon, the menu—Swiss steak, chicken and noodles, fish and meatloaf—was promoted via sandwich signs and barkers waving canes. A year after opening the cafeteria, the men

also began selling beef burgers and lemonade from a 10- by 10-foot no-name tent southwest of the Administration Building. Although the cafeteria closed in 1972, the tent graduated to a trailer with a name—Carl's Beef Burgers. Plus, Mr. Cardamon added hot dogs and invented the gizmo, a mixture of Graziano Brothers sausage and ground beef. Now 81, Mr. Cardamon has turned the business over

"I did doctor up the gizmo sauce a little," says Ms. Wood, adding that it was okay with her father "because I made it even better."

to his daughter and son-in-law, Carla and Kirby Wood of Des Moines. But he's still around during the Fair to make sure everything's okay. "I did doctor up the gizmo sauce a little," says Ms. Wood, adding that it was okay with her father "because I made it even better."

If beef is what's for dinner, members of the Iowa Cattlemen's Association cook up a storm at Cattlemen's Beef Quarters north of the Horse Barn. Since 1985, about 1,100 Association members have committed to feeding 60,000 fairgoers a year every year. And we mean committed! A cattleman or cattlewoman in Dubuque will get up at 2 A.M., drive to the Fair, work for six hours, then drive back home to do chores.

Maybe you want an Iowa chop, instead. In 1999, a cast of thousands lined up for 17,000 Iowa chop-baked beans-applesauce-and-chips sit-down dinners. Thing was, lots of them were lined up before Iowa Pork Producers Association workers flipped back the flaps on the Iowa Pork Tent at 10 in the morning. (Hey, by then it's noon somewhere!)

If you want to munch while meandering, buy something on a stick. How about the "walking chop"—a bone-in, Frenched rib chop. (The bone's the stick.) Or try a turkey leg—a mass of meat first smoked off-site, then crisped up at the Fair about the time you show up hungry at the booth. Actually, you don't so much eat a turkey leg as you gnaw on it, first this side then that. Or go for the classic: Iowa's Grilled Turkey Tenderloin sandwich. When you've polished yours off, ask one of the Iowa Turkey Federation volunteers for a copy of the recipe.

Sticks at the Fair hold just about everything except tossed salad. There's chicken-on-a-stick. Or sausage, bologna, pickles, caramel apples, cheese, and ice cream dipped in chocolate and then in nuts and pretzels. And then there's the King of Stick Food, the corn dog—a hot dog wrapped in sweet cornmeal batter, then plunged into a cauldron of sizzling grease and handed over piping hot. (Not necessarily low-cal, but this is the Fair!)

Actually, that little hot dog is a story in itself. The tale begins with Bob and June Puckett of Des Moines. While visiting her parents in Memphis back in the '40s, they saw a sign advertising pronto pups, decided it might be fun to sell them at the Iowa State Fair, ordered pronto pup batter mix, paid $25 and opened a stand at the next Iowa State Fair. "The first day, we had so much business we couldn't keep the grease hot," Mrs. Puckett remembers.

Success aside, the Pucketts' business only lasted a few years. "It was a hassle," she says, although their stand was next to the Little Train, which daughter Linda got to ride all day long.

Ah, but for the rest of the corn dog story, let's go back to around 1915. That's when Melvin Little's family established Little's Concessions, now Campbell's Concessions. (At one time, the Littles owned and operated as many as 17 cookhouses and beer joints on the Grand Concourse.) In the mid-50s, the hot-dog-on-a-stick seemed to be popping up everywhere, so Mr. Little rolled out his version, called the poncho dog. Daughter Helen, then a teenager, stood inside one of the Littles' stands and shouted, "Get your educated poncho dog! Rides a stick, swims in grease, and wears an overcoat. You bite it; it won't bite you!" Her pitch must have worked because

today the Littles are still selling corn dogs at the rate of 100,000 at their 12 locations during each Fair.

So, the question becomes: Who gets credit for the incredibly successful corn dog? The Pucketts, because they first brought the batter-fried hot dog to the Fair, or the Littles, because they're *still* hawking those dogs? Or does it matter? Probably not, as long as you can get a corn dog at the Fair!

As long as we're talking about credit, when it comes to feeding folks at the Fair, Elston Hardenbrook's family deserves credit for longevity.

Back in 1913, his grandmother, Mary, opened a cook tent where the Cattle Barn now stands. When the Barn eventually opened, it

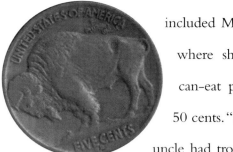

included Mrs. Hardenbrook's Dining Hall, where she served family-style, all-you-can-eat pork, beef and fish dinners for 50 cents. "Sometimes, my uncle had trouble getting dishwashers," says Elston Hardenbrook. "So he'd go down to the drunk tank at the Police Station—he was a police detective—and hire fellows as they got out of jail. They'd work all day, get paid, buy a bottle of wine and end up in the drunk tank. The next day, my uncle would go down when they were getting out and hire them again!"

Mrs. Hardenbrook operated the restaurant and two food stands until 1959. By then, she was 78 years old and ready to retire. So she sold the restaurant and the food stands. Campbell's Concessions now operates the restaurant, called Campbell's Cafe; Elston's father also bought another food stand, which Elston operates. We figure it wouldn't be a Fair without a Hardenbrook food stand!

There are 96 other concessionaires who operate the 185 food stands at the Fair—from American to Mexican, Italian, Chinese, German, Dutch… Such a mix of international foods in the middle of Iowa is no longer surprising. But that doesn't mean there are no more surprises.

For example, now you can get a fried candy bar. That's a bit surprising!

TALK ABOUT A BIG BABY!

In 1929, Iowa's children sent in their nickels and dimes to purchase a baby elephant for the Fair. It weighed 1,160 pounds and was four feet tall. The day it was christened Baby Mine, 25,000 children showed up for the event. That's a lot of kids, but this was, after all, their elephant. The ceremony consisted of pouring a bag of popcorn over Baby Mine's head.

The Iowa State Fair Board and *The Des Moines Register*, cosponsors of the project, apparently had not considered a couple of things: First, elephants require year-round accommodations, including warmth in the winter. Second, baby elephants grow to be adults. Baby Mine's weight doubled, then tripled. "The darn critter {is} eating a bale of hay a day. She {is} eating us out of house and home," said a Fair official. Consequently, in 1942, the board sold Baby Mine to a circus for $750 and donated the money to the polio clinic at Iowa Lutheran Hospital in Des Moines.

Six months before the State Fair opens, Marketing Director Kathie Swift works 40 hours a week. Six weeks before the Fair opens, she works 60–70 hours a week. During the Fair, she has no idea how many hours she works. She says, "If you stop for some reason during the Fair...well, it's just not a good idea to stop during the Fair. You just pour yourself more Gatorade® and keep going."

MARKETING THE FAIR

Talk about a change in culture! Back in the 1850s, the ISAS enticed Iowans to the Fair by promising an event that would "embody into practical, material form, the ideas which would else exist only in the mind as theories." These days, the Fair Board promises us the Fair will be "The Only Fun of Its Kind."

An improvement, right? Still, it wasn't until 1965 that anybody thought to help marketing along by attaching a theme to the Fair. That year, the board launched a series of Heritage Fairs. Each Fair focused on a different era in Iowa history, and each year a major addition was made to the newly created Heritage Village. For example:

• For the Indian Heritage Fair (up to 1800), two wick-i-ups where Woods Indians lived were constructed by George Youngbear and fellow Mesquaki tribesmen from Tama.

• For the Explorer Heritage Fair (1800–1830), a replica of the Fort Madison blockhouse and a section of stockade (the first west of the Mississippi) were built from Iowa oak.

253

• For the Pioneer Heritage Fair (1830–1865), First Church, built in Dubuque in 1834, was re-created. The original was, appropriately, the first church in Iowa. Hymn sings are conducted daily during the Fair.

• For the Gay '90s Fair (1865–1900), the one-room North Lincoln Country School was donated and moved from southeast of Indianola to the fairgrounds by Howard W. Lester, a graduate. An authentic recitation bench and early primers are in the room.

• The Roaring '20s Fair (1900–1930) had folks flappin' to some sweet Dixieland jazz. And the restored Pioneer Hall, encompassing a half-acre of Iowa artifacts, was re-opened to the public.

After celebrating the past, we discovered the present, kicking off the series with Discover Iowa in 1970. The following year, Secretary Ken Fulk decided on Discover Mexico, explaining, "I didn't think we should discover Missouri." (Missouri is our competition!) The spotlight came back to Iowa in 1976, when the State Fair took 12 days to celebrate the country's Bicentennial as well as the "Spirit of Iowa." Iowa ethnic groups like Duane Pichelman's Polka Band and international visitors like the Northumbrian Dancers from England and Ballet Folklorica Mexicano performed. Topping it off was plenty of grand Grandstand entertainment, including Johnny Cash. (It's tough to get more American than Johnny Cash!)

Today, the Fair's themes are just plain funky. "So Much to Go For," "Take a Closer Look" and "Knock Yourself Out" are probably not marketing slogans the ISAS directors would have pinned on their Fairs back in the 1800s. But then, the Society didn't have a Marketing Department to brainstorm themes, discuss pros and cons and ask questions like: How will this theme work in advertising copy? Will it help our competitive exhibitors and concessionaires?

A LITHOGRAPH, BUT NOT IN TIME

It began simply enough. The ISAS wanted a lithograph of the Clinton County Fairgrounds to promote the 1868 Fair. The committee intended to work with a Cincinnati firm noted for its first-class work but was asked to work instead with the Chicago Lithographing Company, even though its reputation was not stellar. Still, the Chicago business manager promised to employ an artist, whose work would be as good as anything you could find in Cincinnati. And so, the Chicago contract was signed.

When the Chicago artist showed up to begin work on the lithograph, he discovered that folks in Clinton and Lyons (the towns bordering the 1868 fairgrounds) also wanted personal lithographs, so he started taking private orders. What he failed to calculate was how much that freelancing was going to cut into his work time and (surprise!) he missed the fairgrounds lithograph deadline.

Perhaps his tardiness could have been overlooked if the lithograph he finally presented was decent, which it wasn't. In fact, the committee declared his work to be "no better than a ten-cent wall-paper and such steamboat and such water—our 'grand river' would have blushed in very shame at the caricature."

Due to time constraints, the ISAS had to use his lithograph. But it must have been bad since the Chicago Lithographing Company not only removed its name from the lithograph but also changed its name to Merchants' Lithographing Company for future business transactions this side of the Mississippi.

SUNDAY AT THE FAIR

At first, the State Fair was three days long, then five, and, finally, it was bumped up to eight in 1882. And no matter how you cut it, one of the eight days was a Sunday.

Not everyone embraced the notion of going to the Fair on a Sunday. A few years earlier, directors of the Centennial Exposition in Philadelphia had decided to remain open on Sunday so workers could attend the World's Fair. That set off a round of protests, which resulted in a compromise: The Fair would operate on Sunday, but all mechanical exhibits must shut down.

So, not surprisingly, the ISAS also found itself smack in the thick of the never-on-Sunday debate. When board member John Scott announced that a Sunday Fair was good for laboring people, someone reminded him that Sunday was for churchgoing. To that, Mr. Scott responded:

"But we are going to have church on the fairgrounds! Talk about church?...You will pay hundreds of dollars to get the best trotting horse here, and with half the money you can have Sunday service conducted by Henry Ward Beecher or DeWitt Talmadge, or [Joseph] Cook...." (Great applause.)

So the ISAS struck a compromise. The Fair would operate on Sunday, but "the more boisterous shows and merchants" must shut down. Additionally, admission would be 25 cents instead of 50 cents. As ISAS Secretary John Shaffer explained:

"Without this admission fee on Sunday, there would doubtless be many who would seek the Fair grounds as a place of idle recreation and careless amusement. With a price charged, this Society has undisputed control of the grounds, and with that control bears the responsibility of a decent observance of the day."

For two decades, religion flourished on the fairgrounds. Orators from as far away as Chicago orated for hours, while thousands listened. There was also music, including Miss Gertrude Haynes of the Story & Clark Organ Concert Company, who played the organ blindfolded.

256

Does it reflect the way we talk? Does it move everyone forward? Does it make everybody from fairgoers to Fair workers feel like they are part of the event? Does it give the Fair a personality?

And finally, does the theme call people to action? The folks who put on the Iowa State Fair don't just want you to *come* to the Fair. They want you to *do* the Fair! Show a lamb or ride the Skyglider. Listen to Inkari play Andean Mountain music or compete with your needlework. Pick up some literature at the Iowa Department of Public Safety or wander around in the General Store. But for heaven's sake, do something! Everybody else is! It's that promise of experience that brings people out to the Fair in record numbers—almost 1 million in 1999.

Want more numbers about the 1999 Fair?

• One million-plus hits from the U.S., Canada, Japan, Australia, Germany, The Netherlands, Norway, United Kingdom, Argentina and Sweden were made on the Fair's Web site (www.iowastatefair.org) during the Fair's run.

• Ridership on the Metro Fair Park 'n' Ride Shuttle was at 101,215.

• Grandstand concert ticket sales grossed $1.2 million. Two sellouts were Goo Goo Dolls and Sugar Ray with Fastball, plus Tim McGraw with Chely Wright.

• Fairgoer ATM withdrawals topped $1,058,000.

LOOKING AHEAD

When our Fair turned 100 in 1954, the Centurlon-Spire of Time was constructed south of the Administration Building. The 20-foot pyramidal structure marks the burial spot for a vault full of artifacts reflective of the '54 Fair: samples of every common seed, feed and fertilizer in use in Iowa; messages addressed to Iowans of 2054 from scores of federal and state government officials and legislators; letters from heads of foreign nations and executives of leading Iowa industrial, professional, agricultural and fraternal organizations; motion picture films and sound recordings; yearbooks and annual reports plus two scores by Fort Dodge composer Karl L. King. The vault will be opened in 2054 during the Bicentennial Iowa State Fair.

Much effort, thought and care went into the selection of those artifacts. And yet, given the opportunity, each of us might have chosen different items to include. That's because the Iowa State Fair is a different experience for each of us, a unique event that becomes solely our own. The Fair—always the same and ever changing—gives to each of us memories and makes to each of us promises. After all these years, what began as an experiment has become an integral part of Iowa's heritage— a slice of life here in the Heartland.

And those of us who love the Fair will forever harbor the treasure of it in our hearts.

SEE WHO IS RUNNING THE SHOW

Iowa State Agricultural Society Secretaries
1854–1902
 Iowa Board of Agriculture
1902–1923
Iowa State Fair Board
1923–present

DR. J.M. SHAFFER
of Fairfield, Iowa
(1854–1856 and 1863–1874)

Even in the days when doctors made house calls, Dr. J.M. Shaffer carved out time for a second "career" with the Iowa State Agricultural Society. He was a founder of the ISAS and served two terms as the secretary of its annual agricultural exposition—the Iowa State Fair. In that position, he fought a myriad of battles: trying to keep the ledger in the black; defining the Fair as a vehicle for education and competition; and debating how entertainment, gambling and liquor (all of which made money) fit into the Fair.

Plus, he found time to participate in the Fair. A report from the first exposition in Fairfield said, "We must here observe that the museum of Dr. J. M. Shaffer attracted a good share of attention. It was composed principally of snakes, lizards, etc., there being upwards of 100—preserved in spirits....The doctor deserves credit for his energy in collecting such a curious assortment."

J.H. WALLACE
of Muscatine, Iowa
(1856–1863)

At the end of Dr. Shaffer's first term as secretary, he was succeeded by J.H. Wallace, a pro-slavery Democrat. Since that was not a popular position for an Iowan, Dr. Shaffer replaced him halfway through the Civil War. Still, Mr. Wallace made his mark. During his first year as secretary, he got the Legislature to up its financial assistance from $1,000 to $2,000. This caused one journalist to report that Mr. Wallace's election was "one of those happy turns of Fortune's wheel, by which the right man is put in the right place... The public is not always wise enough to retain such administrative abilities, when found."

J.R. SHAFFER
of Fairfield, Iowa
(1874–1894)

At the end of Dr. Shaffer's second term, he lobbied the ISAS Board to replace him with his nephew, J.R. Shaffer. There was one other candidate, outgoing ISAS President Col. John Scott. Mr. Scott was an eminent agriculturist; J.R. Shaffer, like his uncle before him, had no agriculture experience. Still, he was elected Fair secretary.

During Mr. Shaffer's first year, the Iowa Agricultural and Mechanical Association was lobbying to bring the Fair to Des Moines. It had purchased land east of the Des Moines River and obtained the backing of *The Iowa State Register* and prominent local residents but still failed in its efforts. Secretary Shaffer didn't think such a move would benefit the ISAS; five years later, he changed his mind, and the Fair landed in Des Moines. And seven years later, in 1886, Des Moines became the Fair's permanent home.

The decision to change proved to be pretty smart. For years, the Society had operated on borrowed money, which made its officers personally liable for the debts. Permanently locating near a city could be an economic boom if you could somehow get all those city folk to attend the agricultural exposition. Mr. Schaffer decided that increasing the entertainment venue could accomplish that. Still, incorporating entertainment into the Fair was controversial, since purists running the show believed its only purpose was educational.

In fact, the entertainment factor led to Mr. Shaffer's decision to leave the secretary's post. In 1893, Iowa was in a depression, the Fair was competing with the Columbian Exposition in Chicago,

and the city of Des Moines was entertaining folks every night with a festival of its own—the destruction of Pompeii via a cardboard volcano and lots of fireworks. Neither the Fair's brass bands nor a balloon ascension complete with a dog and woman who parachuted in front of the Grandstand could match that, and the Society's gate receipts were so low that it couldn't pay its premiums. The '93 Fair plunged the ISAS $25,000 in debt.

The ISAS president said he hoped future volcanic destructions wouldn't occur during the Fair, "for I am confident that it took at night many thousands of dollars which, had it not been here, would have come to us during the day."

Mr. Shaffer, who oversaw all of this, did not run for re-election.

ARGONNE POST BAND

P.L. FOWLER
of Des Moines, Iowa
(1894–1899)

Too bad aspirin wasn't common in the 1890s, because P.L. Fowler could have used some. Every year of his tenure was a challenge:

1894: He inherited an exposition that was $25,000 in debt, so the first thing he did was tell the Legislature that if it didn't pony up with some cash, there'd be no 1894 Fair. The Legislature appropriated less than what was requested, plus torrential rains during the last two days of the Fair washed out gate receipts. A $16,000 debt remained after the bills were paid.

1895: While ISAS members blamed Des Moines for not supporting the financially-beleaguered Fair, everybody else blamed the ISAS. One letter-writer suggested that the "Fair wouldn't be in financial trouble if its officers had any object in view but their own private gain." Obviously, turning a profit was imperative, so Mr. Fowler decided to go after entertainment, despite the controversy. "My idea," he said, "is to have something going on all the time and have so much they cannot see it all in one day and will have to come back." That year, the debt dropped to $10,700.

1896: The ISAS booked Joseph S. Connolly of Des Moines, who staged a colossal collision between two locomotives. Afterward, the ISAS reported, "This closed the Fair for the greatest day ever witnessed

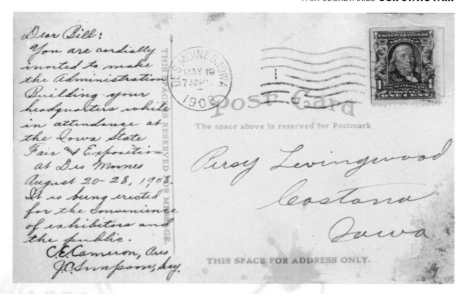

on the Iowa State Fairgrounds; no accidents, and the people went to their homes perfectly satisfied that they had witnessed the most sensational attraction ever put on…." Maybe, but the Fair's debt shot back up to $15,000.

1897: This time, Mr. Fowler put together an "Up-to-Date Fair," which included everything from diving horses to trick shooting. And bingo! The Fair ended up $49 to the good!

1898: Still, $49 wasn't that much even then, so the ISAS asked the city of Des Moines for assistance. When no assistance was forthcoming, the ISAS cancelled the '98 Fair. It need not have bothered; one week later, the United States declared war on Spain, and the state converted the fairgrounds into a military encampment.

G.H. VAN HOUTEN
of Lenox, Iowa
(1899–1901)

G.H. Van Houten's stint as secretary was brief but busy. His first Fair was the last of the century—and last events in any century call for a celebration. So, Mr. Van Houten named that Fair the "Closing Century Exposition," and built it around historical exhibits showing Iowa's aggressive development of agriculture from pioneer times to the beginning of the 20th century.

His last Fair, the final one under ISAS management, locked horns with the weather. Up until the Fourth of July, the weather had never been better. The crops, pastures, flocks and herds all looked great,

and Iowans had every reason to anticipate a prosperous year. Then, hot, blasting winds replaced the rain. Crops withered; flocks and herds dwindled. After much discussion about whether to even hold the Fair, management gave it the thumbs up. Attendance was large, and while some exhibits were not up to par because of the drought, others such as the cattle, swine, sheep, dairy and poultry exhibits "surpassed anything ever seen on the grounds." In the end, *The Farmers Tribune* pronounced it a grand success.

J.C. SIMPSON
of Des Moines, Iowa
(1901–1911)

J.C. Simpson was worth every penny of the $1,500 he earned a year. Just look at his "to-do" list:

1. Build a Livestock Pavilion and Grandstand, Swine and Horse Barns, and the Agriculture, Administration and Varied Industries Buildings.

2. Provide entertainment. Mr. Simpson believed the Fair's purpose was to educate. "Thinking men and women who keep their eyes and the avenues of their brain open understand that education of the farm folk is still the underlying idea of the State Fair," he said. Still, entertainment paid the bills!

3. Suggest the General Assembly do as much for the beautification of the fairgrounds as nature has already done.

4. Fireproof the Grandstand. Mr. Simpson recalled a Wednesday afternoon, a packed Grandstand and fire in an eating house to the east. All the audience

On August 12, 1935, he found three sticks of dynamite on his front porch when he went out to get the morning paper. There was a burned fuse on the front lawn, which investigators believed had been dragged there in the night by the Coreys' German police dog. This was quite possible since Peanuts wasn't fond of anything that smelled like smoke (including a few hands that were holding cigarettes at the time).

The union feud eventually led to a blackout one night during the Fair. Someone from the electrical department had warned that it was planned. So, soon after every light on the east side of Des Moines went out, flashlights lit up the stock pavilion to keep horses from stampeding, candles lit up the offices like a church and two clowns chattered on in front of the Grandstand crowd while Karl King's orchestra played nonstop for 48 minutes. And then, the lights came back on.

They just don't make folks like Mr. Corey any more!

could see was a vast volume of black smoke. That was bad enough, but when people outside began crying "Fire!" the uneasy feeling amounted to almost a panic.

5. Install entrance turnstiles. Cover the streets with cinders. Add sidewalks, more curbs, gutters and storm sewers. Put up wire fencing. Reshingle the barns. Paint the buildings. Construct an imposing Grand Avenue entrance. Install a telephone system.

6. Improve eating conditions. Most dining halls belonged to private parties and were unsightly. "We cannot call to mind any one thing which would be more appreciated by those attending the Fair than to provide a few additional dining halls where a good, wholesome meal could be secured," he said.

With that to-do list, no wonder Mr. Simpson moved to Minnesota in 1911 to run that State Fair.

A.R. COREY
of Des Moines, Iowa
(1911–1941)

While the Legislature was in session, A.R. Corey's kids were never sure when he'd show up for dinner. Dad was on the Hill, lobbying for funds to build the Education Building or the Girls 4-H Dormitory or— the list goes on and on. He engineered a massive

building program, always keeping his eye on a master plan to utilize the fairgrounds' impressive Exposition-style architecture.

But Mr. Corey was also a showman. He replaced pageants with thrill shows, including one they're still talking about: the day back in 1937 when Captain F.F. "Bowser" Frakes crashed his plane into a flimsy house on the infield. Deliberately crashing a plane was illegal, which Mr. Corey and Captain Frakes most likely knew; if they didn't, Major Lester Orcutt of the Commission of Aeronautics showed up at the fairgrounds that morning to tell them. As the story goes, Mr. Corey instructed the Grandstand gate captains not to let the major in until Captain Frakes' plane was flying low across the Midway. The major saw the crash, followed by an ambulance speeding onto the infield, picking up the body next to the fuselage and rushing out of the fairgrounds. Imagine his surprise, then, when authorities stopped the ambulance and discovered that the person inside was neither injured nor Mr. Frakes.

They say Bowser Frakes quietly slipped out of Iowa—maybe with a little help from some of his Fair friends.

Obviously, Mr. Corey didn't back away from much, including problems with the electrical union.

LLOYD CUNNINGHAM
of Cresco, Iowa
(1941–1962)

No doubt about it. Lloyd Cunningham made his mark as secretary. During his tenure, the Fair closed down for four years because of World War II, celebrated its first centennial, grew from eight to 10 days, and reflected the beginnings of agriculture's technological revolution. It was also during this time that the mural came down.

The mural?

Yes, the mural. Painted in 1938 by Dan Rhodes and Howard Johnson, the WPA (Works Progress Administration) project hung in the Agriculture Building. It was 1,100 feet of painting on wood, commemorating Iowa's accession as a federal territory—and it was controversial from the beginning. For example, a man was sowing grain with his left hand, and in 1938, being left-handed was considered a deficit. People also felt that, in general, the men and women in the mural looked "too hard." But the biggest issue probably was that Mr. Rhodes was a regionalist. And in the late '30s, intellectuals still believed that the center of the art world was Paris; consequently, they rejected anything that didn't have an international flair.

Folks needn't have fussed so much. In 1946, the Board gave approval to Secretary Cunningham's request that workmen saw up the $13,000 mural and use the lumber for patchwork around the fairgrounds. After all, Mr. Cunningham didn't like the mural and he needed the lumber.

You won't be surprised to learn that this raised a brief storm of protest. Still, Mr. Cunningham was unrepentant. "The mural wasn't art," he said. "It was WPA. It was an insult to Iowa farmers because it depicted them as club-footed, coconut-headed, barrel-necked and low-browed. Those guys did not look like farmers to me."

The Democratic Party State Chairman, Jake More, blasted Mr. Cunningham. "An investigator whom I sent to see the destruction says a portion of the painting of [Indian Chief] Black Hawk was lying face down on the floor," Mr. Moore declared. "...other pieces of the painting had been nailed along the walls to fill up niches in the new woodwork and used as covers or roofs of booths and stairway arches."

Des Moines Register reporter George Mills eventually took Mr. Cunningham to the Des Moines Art Center to get his opinion on paintings there. Asked what he thought of an abstract painting titled "Guitar with Fruit," the Fair secretary replied, "If that is fruit, it is indigestible. That picture doesn't mean anything to me at all. Either my imagination isn't fully developed or my art education has been neglected."

KEN FULK
of Clarinda , Iowa
(1962–1977)

Ken Fulk planned to serve as secretary for five years but stayed 14 because he kept having "so darn much fun!" (His words.) Plus, he got so darn much done! (Our words.)

For example, he noticed fairgoers constantly dodging cars on Grand Avenue. It certainly was the busiest street on the grounds, what with seven lanes of traffic that funneled to two by the time you reached the main gate. Mr. Fulk's solution? Ban cars and turn Grand Avenue into a beautiful (and safe) Grand Concourse.

Mr. Fulk also thought it was too bad campers had to walk up the big hill to go "home." So he mentioned the need for a shuttle system during a speech to the Clearfield Lions Club. That sounded like a good idea to the club, which has been operating the shuttle since 1964. The Clearfield (population 500) Lions Club (membership 150) runs eight free shuttles daily from 8 A.M. until midnight during the Fair.

Mr. Fulk also spotlighted Iowa history through Heritage Fairs. The totem pole in Heritage Village

was erected for the 1965 Indian Heritage Fair. The pole had been a 400-year-old, 10-ton Idaho-Oregon pine. (It was growing when Columbus discovered America!) It cost $500 to purchase and another $500 to transport from eastern Oregon to the Cattle Barn, where Dick Bordwell of Belle Plaine, his wife, son and daughter carved it up for 40 days (and pretty much 40 nights). The night before the pole was to be lowered into its concrete-and-steel base, Mr. Fulk had his beautiful but very old Dalmatian put to sleep and buried at the base. Mr. Fulk says it is the largest monument any dog in Iowa ever had.

Mr. Fulk also knew that the Fair had been losing about $20,000 a year on weeknight Grandstand entertainment, so he decided to try getting big-name entertainment (a new concept). He asked Des Moines piano teacher Cornelia Hurlbut to invite her nephew and Iowa native, Andy Williams, to perform. For five night shows, Mr. Williams would

receive whatever the Grandstand income was, up to $60,000, then split the rest with the Fair. In the end, he took home $80,000, and the Fair got another $20,000!

But it is the livestock shows of which Mr. Fulk is most proud. He developed rules and methods for a more objective showing of livestock, and as farm numbers shrunk, the number of animals exhibited increased from 8,135 to more than 13,000, making our exhibition the largest in the nation.

J.D. (JIM) TAYLOR
of Parkston, South Dakota
(1977–1986)

As Jim Taylor describes steps taken to ensure a financially sound Fair, it doesn't seem like he's talking about money. It's more like he's weaving one rich memory into another, and you can only conclude that those were invigorating times of change. After all, his term is when free entertainment on the

grounds became commonplace and a master plan to make the Fair self-sufficient and restore aging buildings sounded doable. That's when the Fair flirted with pari-mutuel wagering and created an in-house public relations staff. That's when racing, music festivals and equine events enticed Iowans to the fairgrounds the *other* 11 months of the year.

"I learned a few lessons in those growth years," Mr. Taylor says. For instance, when University Avenue was to be widened, he learned that replanting stately pines wouldn't work, but planting young trees would. So the Fair began planting 100 to 200 trees a year. Today, the Blue Ribbon Foundation offers two programs—Trees for the Fair and Legacy Trees. Mr. Taylor also learned that an extended auto-racing season required a noise ordinance to keep the neighbors happy. And best of all, he learned that Willie Nelson is one great guy.

One year, Mr. Nelson was the Grandstand head-liner. Problem was, it had been raining all day and the opening act refused to go on stage because of the mix of electricity and water. Says Mr. Taylor, "Even though two-thirds of Willie's fans were six-packed to the wind, whooping and hollering, Willie's agent said his man was not going on in the rain." Period.

Dejected, Mr. Taylor asked the booking agent to tell Willie there wasn't going to be a show. "What's going on here?" Mr. Nelson asked when the agent and Mr. Taylor showed up at his trailer door. "We're gonna work!" And with that, he left the trailer, walked on stage and sang for two hours and 25 minutes. (The rain ended after his first song.) His agent was paid in cash—enough $5s, $10s and $20s to make $50,000, which is a lot of money to stick in your boots and down your shirt sleeves, but he managed.

Oh, okay—one more story: Once Mr. Taylor and then-Governor Robert Ray competed in a harness race. "They gave me a 17-year-old horse and they gave Governor Ray a 5-year-old filly that was chomping at the bit," says Mr. Taylor, who lost.

MARION LUCAS
of Montgomery City, Missouri
(1986–present)

Marion Lucas says you can put our State Fair up against anybody else's and we'll come out on top. And he knows why:

• We're still an agricultural fair. "The increasing popularity of private livestock shows has removed the ag component from some state fairs," he says. "Once you lose that component, all you become is an amusement park."

• We're a *diversified* agricultural fair." Today's Iowa is more than cattle and hogs, corn and beans," Mr. Lucas says." So we bring in something a little different every year—a focus on the growing equine industry or an emphasis on the big numbers in sheep or the poten-tial for a grape market. If we feature wine exhibits at the State Fair, maybe Iowans will grow grapes."

• We educate. "We have terrific involvement from FFA and 4-H," he says. "We've maintained high numbers because the youth learn here." But educa-tion isn't limited to the kids—which is why the grape market should be explored.

• We entertain. Unlike the Fair's founding fathers, Mr. Lucas knows a successful fair educates and entertains. "Unfortunately, that entertainment com-ponent gets tougher every year," he says. "Many entertainers who used to play the state fair circuit now perform in 'sheds' like Hilton and won't play an outdoor venue anymore."

• We provide free entertainment. In 1985, 600,000 came to the Fair, and the free entertain-ment budget was $60,000. In 1999, approximately 950,000 came to the Fair, and the free entertainment budget was $400,000. If you fiddle around long enough on your cal-culator, you'll find that it cost less than $1 per person to entice 350,000 more folks to come to the Fair in 1999. "We think the free entertainment had a lot to do with that," Mr. Lucas says.

• We're good-looking! Mr. Lucas has been busy remod-eling and rebuilding what Secretary J.C. Simpson start-ed in 1902. "Quite frankly," Mr. Lucas says, "the Grand-stand was a nightmare. We were hoping $3 million would cover the expenses; we spent $9 million, and we're still not done. But we'll live with what we have."

• We know how to eat! "As I travel the U.S., I can honestly say that we have the best food, bar none!" Mr. Lucas boasts. "You don't see an Iowa chop at every fair."

So what could Mr. Lucas possibly wish for? "More exhibit buildings since we can't fill the requests we receive," he says. "And more room to grow in general. We're running out of places to park cars."

Ah, the growing pains of success!

Marion Lucas

MIGHTY FINE MAINTENANCE SUPERINTENDENTS

When the Iowa State Agricultural Society sponsored its first State Fair in 1854, the ISAS board members were also the superintendents of buildings and grounds (now known as plant operations directors). They built a substantial straight rail fence around the grounds, a shed (with a table inside), 130 stalls, 60 rail pens, a track with a rope guard around it, an office and a stand in the center of the enclosure for the speakers, the chief marshal and the committees.

Of course, between then and now, the superintendent's responsibilities have expanded into an official job description: maintaining and upgrading the existing facilities and overseeing the construction of new ones. But it wasn't until 1890 that we had an official superintendent.

JAMES DEEMER
1890–1920

Mr. Deemer and his family lived in the eight-bedroom home on the fairgrounds that originally had belonged to Calvin Thornton, a cabinetmaker and farmer. The state had purchased land for a permanent fairgrounds from Mr. Thornton in 1884, and the house and barn (today, Grandfather's Barn) were included. The superintendent's family still lives in the Thornton home today.

The big house became a hotel of sorts during State Fair time when members of the State Board of Agriculture and, later, the State Fair Board stayed there. What with all that company, Mr. Deemer and his family simply moved to the attic. Many of the

permanent buildings we use today were constructed during this period, which would have made Mr. Deemer a very busy man. And apparently a good example for his son Edward. He went on to become the Superintendent of Buildings and Grounds at the Minnesota State Fair.

TALKING TO EMPLOYEES NOT PERMITTED. Make all Inquiries Of Sup't. 1933

HENRY DEETS
1921–1961

By the early '20s, the Fair's land and buildings were worth $1 million. There was money set aside for maintenance, but that wouldn't cover big projects such as roof replacement. Since the Fair continued to grow, there was always a call for new construction. So we expect that Henry Deets spent a lot of time during his 40-year tenure stretching dollars.

Even so, he obviously did not lose his sense of humor. Consider the Night Watchman Story which involved Mr. Deets, his friend Clarence Danley and Charlie Day, the Fair's night watchman.

Mr. Deets' office was in the Cattle Barn when the Fair wasn't in session. Each evening, Mr. Day

patrolled the grounds on horseback; often, he'd tie up his horse by the Cattle Barn and go visiting for awhile. One particular time while the watchman was off chatting, Mr. Deets and Mr. Danley took the saddle off his horse and led it away. Then, they saddled up a plaster of Paris display horse used by the Boyt Harness Company during the Fair. (The rest of the year, the horse stood by quietly in Grandfather's Barn.)

Next, Mr. Deets went to another area of the fairgrounds and called in a fire alarm. When the alarm sounded, it's said that Mr. Day ran out of the barn, jumped on his mount and kicked it in the flanks. Ouch!

FLOYD DEETS
1961–1985

When Henry retired, son Floyd took over. He knew the fairgrounds well, having been born and raised there. (Once during those growing-up years, Floyd gave his pony and donkey a tour of inside of the family home. Need we mention that his parents were away at the time?)

For this Mr. Deets, maintenance issues and money were critical. The Fair was expanding, facilities were being used year-round, and there was construction as well as destruction. Continued funding at current levels might require the Fair Board to close down some structures. Most likely, Mr. Deets became even more adept at stretching those dollars than his father had been before him.

Still, all his challenges weren't major. Once, a *Des Moines Tribune* columnist asked why he wasn't spraying the fields of dandelions on the Fairgrounds. No money, no permission, he said. Besides, folks came out and picked the greens to make dandelion wine. One day, Superintendent Deets overheard a woman exclaiming to her friends, "My husband is going to love me for this! I have 40 cents worth of dandelions and $9 worth of dew worms!"

In those days, the Grandstand seats were round-back oak chairs bolted onto boards—eight to a board. Each spring, Mr. Deets and his crew hauled the chairs out of the mezzanine and set them up for the season. After the Fair, Mr. Deets and his crew put the chairs back in storage. Which all sounds fairly simple until you realize that we're talking about 12,000 chairs.

BILL HARE
1986–present

Bill Hare showed up during better times. While Floyd Deets had to squeeze every penny (they straightened nails for reuse), Legislative appropriations and Blue Ribbon Foundation money enabled Mr. Hare's crew to use new nails. Restoration projects, new construction and complementing projects, such as new restrooms, shower houses and landscaping, have kept Mr. Hare's crew of 25 busy all the time.

Still, there was that one day in the late '90s when Dick Curry quit working for a bit. It was right after an Iowa snowstorm, and the blade on Mr. Curry's plow had inadvertently knocked the cover off the manhole in front of the WHO Crystal Studio. When Mr. Curry climbed down to replace the cover, he glanced into the manhole and saw a body (at least, it *looked* like a body). "That was about as bad a piece of news as I could get," said Mr. Hare, who knew he had to go check it out. At first, Mr. Hare couldn't see anything because it was light outside and dark inside. So he got down on hands and (weak) knees, and sure enough, it seemed there was somebody down there in coveralls.

The "body" turned out to be a big ball of brush, debris and rags that looked a lot like clothing—making it one of those incidents you could laugh about later on. "When I first came to work here, I heard all those stories about people disappearing on the Fairgrounds," says Mr. Hare. "And that winter morning when I was looking in the manhole, all those stories came back to me."

To date, Mr. Hare and his staff haven't found any fairgrounds ghosts. But then, they aren't out there looking for them, either!

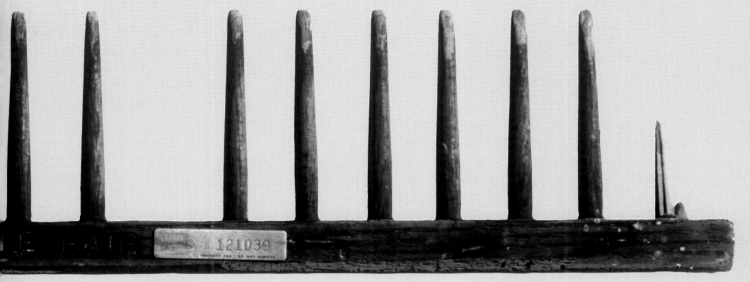

Left to Right: Robert Schlutz; Bob Miller; Bill Partlow; Paul Vaassen; Marion Lucas, Secretary/Manager; Bill Neubrand; Don Greiman, President; David Huinker, Vice-President; Leona Ashman; C.W. Thomas; Randy Brown (front); John (Mel) Shanda, Treasurer (inset)

THE IOWA STATE FAIR BOARD

Don Greiman of Garner remembers way back to when he was a little boy spending time with his mother in the Women and Children's Building while his father, a purebred Angus breeder, was in the Cattle Barn. At those long-ago State Fairs, he ate two ice cream cones a day—a big treat during the Depression—plus dinner at a church stand and, finally, supper at Mrs. Hardenbrook's Dining Hall in the Cattle Barn before heading home.

He says showing the Grand Champion 4-H Angus breeding heifer in 1947 was "at the time, the biggest thrill of my life. And the icing on the cake was a Hamilton wristwatch from *Wallaces Farmer* for being top beef showman." (The watch doesn't run anymore, but he still has it!)

Mr. Greiman didn't know it then, but his involvement with the Fair was just beginning. While an animal husbandry major at Iowa State College, he worked in the Fair's 4-H beef department. As a young farmer, he raised and exhibited purebred beef cattle and traveled the country, judging beef shows. Then, one day in 1965, Fair Secretary Ken Fulk called Mr. Greiman and said, "Don, you're running for the Iowa State Fair Board. You need to be in Des Moines for the convention because that's when we have the election."

Good thing Mr. Greiman went to the convention, because he won a seat on the board. It's a seat he still occupies today.

The Fair Board was established by the Legislature in 1923. Prior to that, the Fair was run through the Iowa Department of Agriculture (1902-1923) and, prior to that, by the Iowa State Agricultural Society. Board members include the governor, secretary of agriculture and president of Iowa State University ex officio, as well as two delegates from each congressional district. Members are paid per diem and reimbursed for expenses with board funds.

The president and vice president are elected by and from its members; the treasurer and manager are appointed by the board. Mr. Greiman served as president from 1977-1980 and again from 1999 to the present. Hands down, his service sets a record!

Officially speaking, the board establishes policies governing the Fair; the premium list; the control of the fairgrounds, including buildings and equipment; the concessions and all other related aspects. Its mission and purpose are to promote Iowa and its products and, in doing so, depict how Iowans live, work and play. In layperson terms, the board deals with just about every aspect of the Fair:

Livestock. The board is proud of the quantity and quality of its competitive and commercial agricultural exhibits. The Fair is considered one of the premier livestock shows in the nation—as it should be, since we're in the middle of the country's livestock and grain-producing areas. Many new breeds and species of livestock and poultry are continually being added to the premium list.

Buildings and Grounds. The board is proud that the original buildings are on the National Register of Historic Places and praises those who laid out the fairgrounds more than 100 years ago. Visiting officials comment on the unique design and location of treasured buildings as well as our remarkable traffic flow pattern. "You don't have a fairgrounds here," one official said. "You have a park."

Commitment to Youth. The board supports youth by offering quality facilities and programs, often made possible through support of interested groups and associations. That's why there's a new FFA Exhibits Building, for example, and why 50-plus scholarships from various organizations are presented during each Fair.

Now you know about the Fair board and how its good work helps make our State Fair a great State Fair. Between 1923, when the State Fair Board was legislated into existence, and the end of the century, attendance soared from 365,755 to 970,000; net profit in 1923 was $54,984, and by 1999, after allowing for depreciation and expenses, the Fair showed a net gain of $482,339; premiums paid climbed from $105,886 in 1923 to $382,100 in 1999.

In that same period, Iowa's population only went from 2,404,000 to 2,860,000.

So next time you see a board member walking down the Grand Concourse, stop, shake hands and say, "Hey, thanks a lot!"

Iowa State Agricultural Society 1860–99

Thomas W. Clagett, Fairfield   Pres. 1854–58
Z.T. Fisher, Oskaloosa   Pres.1859
W.W. Hamilton, Dubuque   VP 1859
Isaiah Booth, Linn Co.   1859
L.W. Babbitt, Pottawattamie Co.   1859
George G. Wright, Keosauqua   Pres.1860–64
Mark Miller, Dubuque   VP 1860–62, (Treas. 1862)
M.L. Morris, Iowa City   1859–61 (Treas. 1860–61)
Dr. T.K. Brooks, Polk Co.   1859–64
J.M. Cannon, Scott Co.   1859–61
Dr. George Sprague, Island Grove, Butler Co.
   1860–61, Treas. 1866–69
H.G. Stuart, Lee Co.   1859–61
Oliver Mills, Lewis, Cass Co.   1860–78
   (Pres. 1874–76)
Dr. J.D. Wright, Marion Co.   1859–64
Peter Melendy, Cedar Falls   1859–69, 1871
   (VP 1863–64) (Pres. 1865–69) (Treas. 1871)
G.W. Kincaid, Muscatine Co.   1859–60
Henry Olmsted, Harrsion Co.   1859–61
Robert Seevers, Oskaloosa   1859–67 (Treas. 1859)
Phineas Caldwell, Magnolia   1862–70, 1872–75
Edwin Smith, Davenport   1862–65, 1868–73
   (Treas. 1863–65) (VP 1872–73)
M.W. Robinson, Burlington   1862–69
E.R. Shankland, Dubuque   1863–69
   Pres.1870–1871
Hiriam Bailey, Chickasaw Co.   1861
O.O. St. John, Chickasaw Co.   1863
W.S. Eddy, Harrison Co.   1862–64
Timothy Day, Winchester   1863–69
S.F. Spofford, Des Moines   1864–71, 1877–78
   (VP 1870–71) (Pres. 1877–78)
James D. Wright, Chariton   1865–69
S.B. Hewitt, Jr., Eagle Grove   1865–74
A.J. Adkison, Winterset   1865
John H. Bacon, Washington   1866–67
C.T. Lamson, Anamosa   1865–66
Milo Smith, Clinton   1867–71
F.L. Downing, Oskaloosa   1868–80 (Pres.1879–80)
C.F. Davis, Keokuk   1870, 1872–75 (Treas. 1870)
P. McIsaacs, Waterloo   1870–73
John Grinnell, Clayton   1870–78 (VP 1877–78)
John Bacon, Washington   1870–71
J.M. Tuttle, Des Moines   1870–71
John Scott, Nevada   1871–73 (Pres. 1872–73)
William B. Leach, Cedar Rapids   1872–73
J.W. Porter, Iowa City   1872–82 (Pres. 1881–82)
M.W. Robinson, Des Moines   1872–76
   (VP 1874–76)
Aaron Kimball, Cresco   1872–74
S.S. Sample, Keokuk   1874–75
C. Close, Cedar Valley   1874–75
E.S. Fonda, Osage   1874–75
S.H. Mallory, Chariton   1874–77
J.J. Snouffer, Cedar Rapids   1874–88 (VP 1886–88)
S.C. Bever, Cedar Rapids   1876–78)
D.M. Flinn, Booneville   1875–77
George C. Duffield, Pittsburg   1876–87
N. S. Ketchum, Marshalltown   1876–79
C.E. Hedges, Sioux City   1876–78
Filch B. Stacy, Stacyville   1876–88
E.N. Clark, Postville   1877–80
James Wilson, Traer   1878–82 (VP 1882)
George H. Wright, Sioux City   1878–79
S.A. Knapp, Vinton   1879–81
C.F. Clarkson, Des Moines   1879 (VP 1879)
J.G. Rounds, Des Moines   1879–83
George Gray, Stuart   1879–82
E.F. Brockway, Ainsworth   1880–81, 1883
   (VP 1880–81, 1883)
L.S. Coffin, Fort Dodge   1880–86
J.T. Beebe, Afton   1880–81
Hiriam C. Wheeler, Odebolt   1881–1888,
   (VP 1884–85) (Pres.1886–88)
R.C. Webb, Des Moines   1881–92

Frank N. Chase, Cedar Falls   1882–94 (VP 1894)
William T. Smith, Oskaloosa   1882–85
   (Pres. 1883–85)
L.C. Baldwin, Council Bluffs   1882–91
J.D. Brown, Leon   1883–90 (VP 1889–90)
L.F. Newell, Agency City   1884–87
H.B. Griffin, Maquoketa   1883–93
George H. Maish, Des Moines   1884–87
   (Treas. 1884–87)
P. Walls, Boone   1887–88
John Hayes, Red Oak   1887–90 (VP 1889–90)
C.B. Worthington, Des Moines   Treas.1888–93
John A. Evans, West Liberty   1888–96
   (VP 1892–93) (Pres. 1894–96)
Ballingall, Ottumwa   1889–90
H.I. Smith   1888–92
J.W. McMullin, Oskaloosa   1889–93
   (VP 1891) (Pres. 1892–93)
C.C. Carpenter, Fort Dodge   1889
W.W. Field, Odebolt   1889–97
   (VP 1895–96) (Pres. 1897)
Albert Head, Jefferson   1891 (Pres. 1891)
*J.P. Manatrey, Fairfield   1892–02 (1st District 1900)
P.L. Fowler, Osceola   1891–93
A.H. Grisell, Menlo   1891
S.S. Sessions, Algona   1890–93
George W. Franklin, Atlantic   1892–93, 1898
Head, Des Moines   Treas.1894
John Cownie, South Amana   1894–98
   (VP 1897) (Pres. Jan–Apr 1898)
*J.C. Frasier, Bloomfield   1894–1901
   (VP 1899–1900) (Pres. 1901)
C.C. Prouty, Des Moines   1893–94
C.H. Bacon, Cromwell   1894–95
B.J. Moore, Missouri Valley   1892–95
Daniel Sheehan, Osage   1893–99
W.F. Harriman, Hampton   1894–98
   (VP Jan–Apr 1898) (Pres. Apr 1898–99)
*R.J. Johnston, Humboldt   1894–1900,
   (VP Apr 1898–99) (Pres. 1900)
*G.D. Ellyson, Des Moines   Treas. 1895–1906
*C.E. Cameron, Alta,   1895–1931 (VP 1902–05)
   (Pres. 1906–31, retired) (11th District 1900)
Ben F. Elbert, Des Moines   1895–97
L.H. Pickard, Harlan   1896–99
*M.J. Wragg, Waukee   1896–05 (7th District 1900)
*J.W. Wadsworth, Algona   1898–04
   (10th District 1900)
A.L. Plummer, Ivy   1898–99
G.L. Johnson, Maquoketa   1898
John Howatt, Welton   1899
*W.W. Morrow, Afton   1899–05, 1915–22
   (VP 1901) (Pres. 1902–05)
   (8th District, 1900) (Treas.1915–22)

State Board of Agriculture (11 Districts) 1900–23

C.W. Phillips, Maquoketa   2nd District 1900–16
W.C. Brown, Clarion   3rd District 1900–09
   (VP 1906–09)
R.T. St. John, Riceville   4th District 1900–07
S.B. Packard, Marshalltown   5th District 1900–08
T.C. Legoe, What Cheer   6th District 1900–23
McDonald, Bayard   9th District 1900–08
R.S. Johnston, Columbus Junction   1st District
   1903–13
John Ledgerwood, Leon   8th District 1901–11
   (VP 1910–11)
Harold L. Pike, Whiting   11th District 1902–56
   (1934 9th District) (1943 7th District)
   (Pres. 1948–56) (resigned)
G.S. Gilbertson, Des Moines   Treas.1907–14
Elmer M. Reeves, Waverly   3rd District 1906–22
E.J. Curtin, Decorah   4th District 1908–26
E.M. Wentworth, State Center   5th District 1909–13

C.F. Curtiss, Ames   7th District 1905–1937
   (6th District 1934)
Chas. Escher, Jr., Botna   9th District1909, 1916–1921
O.A. Olson, Forest City   10th District 1905–18
   (VP 1911–18)
Frank Sheldon, Mt. Ayr   1910–46, 8th District
   (Treas. 1922–31) (VP 1932–46)
John F. Summers, Malvern   9th District 1910–15
John P. Mullen, Fonda   10th District 1911–47
   (VP 1918–31) (Pres. 1932–47) (retired)
C.H. Tribby, Mt. Pleasant   1st District 1914–17
Cyrus A. Tow, Norway   5th District 1914–24
E.T. Davis, Iowa City   2nd District 1917–48
   (1st District 1934)(retired)
H.O. Weaver, Wapello   1st District 1918–33

Iowa State Fair Board 1924-Present

Earl Ferris, Hampton   3rd District 1922–33
Ed Beaman, Oskaloosa   6th District 1922–41
   (5th District 1934)
J.C. Beckner, Clarinda   8th District 1922–33
C.E. Hoffman, Atlantic   9th District 1922–41
   (7th District 1934)
Sears McHenry, Denison   10th District 1919–38
   (8th District 1934)
E.J. Knickerbocker, Fairfax   5th District 1925–39
   (2nd District 1934)
Paul Stewart, Maynard   4th District 1927–35

(Redistricted to 9 Districts, 1934)

N.W. McBeath, Whiting   Treas.1932–57 (resigned)
L.B. Cunningham, Cresco   4th District 1936–40
   (became Secretary in 12/40)
W.H. Maxwell, Winterset   6th District 1938–57
   (5th District 1934)
Paul P. Zerfass, Algona   8th District 1938–41

(Redistricted to 8 Districts, 1941)

William J. Campbell, Jesup   2nd District 1940–59
   (1947–56) (Pres. 1956–60) (resigned)
P.K. Wright, Iowa Falls   3rd District 1940
C.S. Macy, Grundy Center   3rd District 1941–61
Sam Carpenter, Centerville   4th District 1943–52
   (retired)
John W. Cory, Jr., Spencer   1942–62, 8th District
   (Pres. 1960–62) (resigned)
Brady O. Gates, Independence   2nd District 1947–48
Ben Doran, Beaver   6th District 1947–50
Lyle R. Higgins, Harlan   7th District 1948–66
   (VP 1956–62) (Pres. 1963–66)
E.W. Williams, Manchester   2nd District 1949–53
Harry M. Duncan, Columbus Junction   1st District
   1949–69 (At-Large 1965)
   (VP 1963–66) (Pres. 1967–69)
C.J. Matthiesson, Monticello   2nd District 1953–76
   (VP 1970–72) (Pres. 1973)
C.C. Wagler, Bloomfield   4th District 1953–76
   (VP 1967–69) (Pres. 1970–72)
   (Treas. 1975–76)
J.H. Kutter, Rockwell City   6th District 1951–62
William J. Hitz, Polk City   Treas. 1957–65
Wilbur Yount, Altoona   5th District 1957–71
   (At-Large 1972) (VP 1973) (Pres. 1974)
W.P. Manatt, Audubon   7th District 1956–61
   (resigned)

(Redistricted to 7 Districts, 1961; 3 Directors at Large, 1965)

Lloyd C. Albers, Spirit Lake   8th District 1960
   (lost district to redistricting, 1961)
Tom Scott, Dallas Center   Treas. 1966–74
Howard Waters, Danville   1st District 1963–76
   (VP 1975) (Pres. 1976)
George E. Janssen, Eldora   3rd District 1962–71
   (resigned)
Jean M. Kleve, Humboldt   6th District 1963–84
   (VP 1974) (Pres. 1975)

Gerald W. Prince, Guthrie Center   7th District1963–78
   (5th District 1972) (VP 1976)
   (Pres. 12/76–1/77)
Don Greiman, Garner   1966–Present
   At-Large 1966–71, 1982–91
   3rd District 1971, 5th District 92–Present
   (VP 12/76–1/77)
   (Pres.1977–80, (2000–Present)
Chas. "Chuck" Iles, Des Moines   At-Large 1967–71

(Redistricted to 6 Districts 1971)

Joe Deeney, Waukon   At-Large 1971–77 (VP 1977)
Edythe Satterlee, Manchester   2nd District 1976–85
   (VP 1978–79)
Max Browneller, Rose Hill   4th District 1976
Merritt Triggs, Mt. Ayr   1976–97, At-Large 1976–79
   5th District 1979 (VP 1981–83)
   (Pres. 1984–86)
John "Mel" Shanda, Perry   Treas. 1977–Present
Ed Eichelberger, West Liberty   1st District 1977–82
   (VP 1980)
Katy Elson, Bondurant   4th District 1977–81
   (resigned)
Fred Strothman, New London   At-Large 1978–86
   (Pres. 1981–83)
Bill Neubrand, LeMars   At-Large 1978–80
   5th District 1992–Present (VP 1998–99)
Clifford Johnson, Elkhorn   At-Large 1979–81
Dave Huinker, Decorah   1980–Present
   At-Large 1980–82
   3rd District/2nd District 1982–Present
   (VP 1987–89, 2000-Present) (Pres. 1991–92)
James A. Rutt, Columbus Junction   1st District
   1982–88
Ed Yelick   4th District 1982–84
Ed Ahrendsen, Audubon   1982–99
   At-Large 1982–91, 4th District 1992–99
   (VP 1984–86) (Pres. 1987–90)
Paul Vaassen, Dubuque   2nd District 1985–Present
   (VP 1990–92) (Pres. 1993–95)
Bill Riley, Des Moines   4th District 1985–87
   (resigned)
Douglas Anderson, Hampton   6th District 1985–91
Robert H. Lounsberry   4th District 1987–90
Gail Danilson, Woodward   At-Large 1986–91

(Redistricted to 5 Districts and no At–Large members, 1992)

Glenn Hughes, Eldon   1st District 1989–91
Bill Partlow, Ankeny   4th District 1991–Present
Robert Schlutz, Columbus Junction   1st District
   1992–Present, (VP 1993–95) (Pres. 1996–97)
Evans Waller, Bennett   1st District 1992–98
Leona Ashman, Oskaloosa   3rd District
   1992–Present
   (VP 1996–97) (Pres. 1998–99)
Max Bishop, Indianola   3rd District 1998–99
Bob Miller, Riverside   1999–Present
Randy Brown, Osceola   3rd District 2000–Present
C.W. Thomas, Guthrie Center   4th District
   2000–Present

PHOTO CREDITS

Photos are attributed clockwise, beginning with A in the upper left corner of the page. BG represents a background photo; FC represents the front cover; BC represents the back cover.

Russ Bickett

All artwork from the Iowa State Historical Society was photographed by Russ Bickett

Lou Christie

Page 130C (copyright 1999 All rights reserved. Reprinted with permission.)

The Des Moines Register and Tribune

Pages 58A (Doug Peterson, copyright 1999); 142B (Doug Wells, copyright 1997); 163C (Gary Fandel, copyright 1991); 165B (Bob Modersohn, copyright 1992); 167A (Charles Schlosser, copyright 1990); 177B (Anne Fitzgerald, copyright 1996); 242B (Bob Modersohn, copyright 1996); 244BG, 245BG, 245A (Bob Nandell, copyright 1999); 245B (Bob Nandell, copyright 1995); 246A (Bob Modersohn, copyright 1996) All rights reserved. Reprinted with permission.

Lesley Gore

Page 130D (copyright 1999 All rights reserved. Reprinted with permission.)

Courtesy of Tom and Beth Greenley

Page 111

Courtesy of Ellen Hammond

Pages BCD, 12D, 30A-31A, 117, 118A, 118B, 142BG-143BG, 143, 205A, 205C, 207C, 208A, 208B, 211C, 225A, 231A, 261A

Jim Heemstra

Pages 7C, 30C-31C, 97B, 147B, 148C, 149C, 158A, 160-161, 174, 181A, 204A, 204B, 212, 259A

Iowa FFA Association

Page 185B

Iowa State Fair Blue Ribbon Foundation

Pages 52A, 88-89 (photo by Dave Popelka, Sigler Printing & Publishing), 168BG-169BG (print by Bill McNarney), 179B (photo by Kelly Laabs), 184 (photo by Dave Popelka, Sigler Printing & Publishing), 187B (print by Frank Champion Murphy), 214C (print by Bill McNarney), 215A (print by Bill McNarney), 230B (photo by Dave Popelka, Sigler Printing & Publishing), 268BG (print by Bill McNarney), 271A, 271B, 271C

Iowa State Fair Museum

Pages FCB, BCI, 6A, 6B, 8-9, 10-11A, 11B, 12B, 16B, 17A, 17B, 18B, 24A, 30B, 32A, 33A, 34, 36, 38, 39A, 39B, 40, 41, 42BG-43BG, 42B, 43A, 43B, 46A, 46B, 47, 52B, 52C, 54B, 60A, 60B, 60C, 60D, 61B, 62A, 62B, 62C, 62D, 63A, 63B, 63C, 64BG, 64A, 66BG, 66A, 68BG, 70-71, 73C, 74BG-75, 77, 78B, 79A, 79B, 80A, 80B, 81BG, 81A, 81B, 81C, 82A, 82B, 85C, 100B, 110A, 110B, 112A, 113B, 115C, 116A, 116B, 120B, 120A, 123B, 123C, 123D, 123E, 124B, 125A, 127A, 127B, 128C, 128D, 128E, 131B, 134B, 136A, 137C, 137D, 152A, 155B, 156B, 156C, 157D, 159D, 163B, 166A, 167D, 168B, 171A, 171C, 171D, 182A, 188B, 189, 190A, 190B, 190C, 192B, 193B, 193C, 193D, 202A, 209A, 209B, 209C, 209D, 209E, 210-211A, 219B, 226, 230A, 239A, 250, 251B, 252B, 253A, 253C, 254, 255, 261B, 262B, 263, 264B, 265A, 266B-267B, 268B

Larassa Kabel

Page 216B

Paul Micich

Pages 12C, 148B, 151A, 15A, 205B, 213 A, 251A

Courtesy of Don Muhm

Page 7E, 7F

Christine Quinn & John Naisbitt

Pages BCJ, 99A, 138, 142A, 200, 220

Lynda Richards

Pages BDF, 3, 12A, 13, 52B, 72C, 92C, 98A, 132-133, 139A, 169A, 172B, 172D, 173B, 173D, 175A, 206A, 206B-207A, 219C, 225B, 246B, 249B, 256, 258A, 268A, 270

Rich Sanders

All images in the book with *cut-out-backgrounds* and many copy images were photographed by Rich Sanders

State Historical Society of Iowa - Des Moines

Pages FCA, BCA, BCB, BCC, BCE, BCG, BGH, BCK, 7A, 7B, 7D, 11C, 14, 15B, 15C, 16-17BG, 16B, 18A, 19, 20-21, 22A, 22B, 22C, 22D, 22E, 23A, 23B, 23C, 23D, 24B-25B, 25A, 26BG-27, 26B, 28-29, 30BG-31BG, 35, 43A, 44A, 44B, 45A, 45B, 48-49, 50-51A, 53A, 53B, 53C, 54A, 55A, 55B, 56, 57, 58B, 59, 60BG-61BG, 61A, 62BG-63BG, 64B, 64C, 65, 66B, 67, 68A, 69A, 69B, 69C, 72A, 72B-73A, 73B, 74A, 76A, 76B, 78A, 82C, 83, 84, 85A, 85B, 85D, 86, 87A, 87B, 90, 91A, 91B, 92A, 92B-93A, 93B, 94-95, 96-97A, 97C, 98B, 99B, 99C, 100A, 101, 102, 103, 104A, 104B, 104C, 105, 106A, 106B, 107BG, 108, 109, 110C, 112B, 113A, 113C, 114BG-115BG, 114A, 114B, 114C, 115A, 115B, 119, 120C, 121BG, 121A, 121B, 121C, 121D, 122-123A, 124BG, 124A, 124C, 125B, 125C, 126A, 126B, 126C, 126D, 127BG, 128A, 128B, 129A, 129B, 129C, 131A, 134A, 134C, 135A, 135B, 136BG-137BG, 136B, 137B, 138BG 139BG, 139B, 140A, 140B, 141A, 141B, 141C, 141D, 141E, 142C, 144-145, 146-147A, 148A, 149A, 149B, 150A, 150B, 151B, 152B, 153A, 153B, 154A-155A, 154B, 155C, 156BG-157BG, 156A, 157A, 157B, 157C, 158B, 159A, 159B, 159C, 162A-163A, 164A-165A, 165C, 166B, 166C, 167B, 167C, 168A, 169B, 169C, 170, 171B, 172A, 172C, 173A, 173C, 175B, 176A-177A, 177C, 178A, 178B-179A, 178B, 179C, 180, 181B, 182B, 183A, 185A, 186A, 186B, 187A, 187C, 188A, 190D, 191, 192A, 193A, 194-195, 196-197, 198, 199, 202B-203, 207B, 211B, 213B, 214A, 214B, 215B, 216-217, 218-219A, 221A, 221B, 222, 223, 224, 227, 228-229, 234, 235A, 235B, 236-237, 238A, 238B, 238C, 239B, 240BG-241BG, 240, 241, 242A, 243, 244, 248A, 248B, 249A, 252A, 252C, 253B, 258BG-259BG, 258B, 258C, 259B, 260A, 260B, 261BG, 262A, 264A, 265B, 267A, 271D

Tribune Media Services

Page 233B (copyright All rights reserved. Reprinted with permission.)

Wallaces Farmer

Page 37

Bill Woolston

Pages 137A, 221C (copyright 1975 All rights reserved. Reprinted with permission.)

State Fair Board Ex-Officio Members

1900	Governor	ISU President	Dairy Commissioner	State Vet.
1900	Leslie M. Shaw	W.M. Beardshear	B.P. Norton	J.I. Gibson
1903	Albert Cummins			
1908	Warren Garst			
1910	Syril Carroll			
1914	George W. Clarke			
1918	William L. Harding			
1919		R.A. Pearson	W.B. Barney	Robert D. Wall
1921	Nathan E. Kendall			Peter Malcolm
			Sec. of Agriculture	
1922			R.W. Cassady	
1924			Mark G. Thornburg	Position gone
1925	John Hammill			
1927		Herman Knapp (Acting)		
1928		R.M. Hughes		
1931	Dan W. Turner			
1933	Clyde L. Herring		Ray Murray	
1936		C.E. Friley		
1937	Nelson G. Kraschel		Thomas L. Curran	
1939	George A. Wilson		Mark G. Thornburg	

1940	Governor	ISU President	Sec. of Agriculture
1943	Bourke Hickenlooper		Harry G. Linn
1945	Robert D. Blue		
1949	William S. Beardsley		
1950			Clyde Spry
1953	Leo Elthon	James Hilton	
1955	Leo A. Hoegh		
1957	Herschel C. Loveless		
1961	Norman A. Erbe		L.B. Liddy
1963	Harold E. Hughes		
1965		W. Robert E. Parks	Kenneth Owens
1967			L.B. Liddy
1968	Robert D. Ray		
1972			Robert Lounsberry
1980			
1983	Terry Branstad		
1986		Gordon Eaton	
1987			Dale Cochran
1990		Milton Glick (Acting)	
1991		Martin Jischke	
1999	Tom Vilsack		Patty Judge

THE "IOWAN OF THE DAY"

Every spring, the Iowa State Fair Blue Ribbon Foundation launches a search for 10 very special Iowans—people who have made significant contributions to their communities and to the state. Additionally, these people exhibit the characteristics associated with Iowa: integrity, dependability, sense of community and a strong work ethic. Come August, each of those 10 becomes an "Iowan of the Day"—one for each of the first 10 days of the Fair. The "Iowan of the Day" is the Fair's honored guest. He or she is introduced on the Bill Riley Stage and given awards, including numerous prizes, a cash award, hotel accommodations provided by the Des Moines Marriott, and a one-year subscription to *The Iowan* magazine. Cookies Food Products is also a sponsor.

The program was started in 1997; a panel of judges selects winners from nominations. Anyone can nominate an Iowa citizen for this honor. Forms are available at local libraries, various volunteer organizations and by contacting the Blue Ribbon Foundation.

"The 'Iowan of the Day' award is a thank-you to the 10 outstanding winners for the work they do to make Iowa such a great place to live," says John Putney, executive director of the Foundation.

1997
Charlie Becker, Monticello
Veronica Ballard, Floyd
Roger Neville, Odebolt
Jean Marquart, Lincoln
William C. Knapp, West Des Moines
Marcella Howe, Creston
Donald F. Lamberti, Ankeny
Claude Ahrens, Grinnell
Judy Badder, Lamoni
Ron Drake, Red Oak

1998
James Sauter, North English
Jean Klingman, Waterloo
Craig Foss, Fairfield
Jan Winslow, Corydon
Rev. Alan Rusk, Clearfield
John Ruan, Des Moines
Betty Brotherton, Wall Lake
Gene Powers, Des Moines
George Mathews, Mason City
Elizabeth Andre, Ames

1999
Barbara Hannon, Bedford
Raymond Butt, Lewis
Dennis Gienger, Gladbrook
Ron Corbett, Cedar Rapids
Gib McConnell, Indianola
Leigh & Dorothy Curran, Mason City
Jane Tornblom, Dubuque
Kris Young, Runnells
Bob Reed, Albia
Natalie Spoo, Glenwood

IOWA STATE FAIR

DES MOINES

See the
Air Ship

W. W. MORROW, Pres't
J. C. SIMPSON, Sec'y

1906

AUGUST

24=31

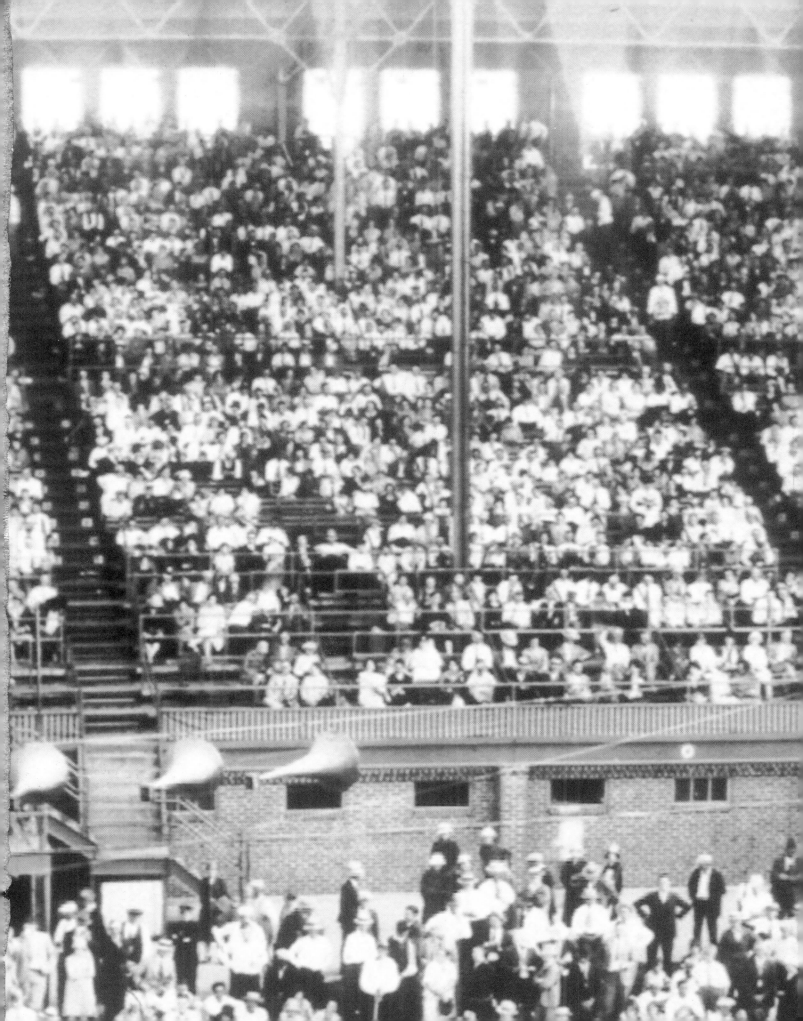